FLOWERS
IN COLOUR

With love
+ Best Wishes
for a Very Happy Birthday
+ many Happy Returns
frae
Meg + Jack.
13. July 1961.

FLOWERS
IN COLOUR

an Amateur Gardening encyclopaedia

BY A. G. L. HELLYER, F.L.S

illustrated from watercolour drawings

BY CYNTHIA NEWSOME-TAYLOR

and from wood engravings

BY J.D.C.SOWERBY, F.L.S

MCMLV

W. H. & L. COLLINGRIDGE LTD LONDON

TRANSATLANTIC ARTS NEW YORK

FIRST PUBLISHED IN 1955
by W. H. & L. Collingridge Limited
2-10 Tavistock Street London W.C. 2
and in the United States of America by
Transatlantic Arts Incorporated New York
Colour plates engraved by
The Sun Engraving Co Ltd London & Watford
and printed by Balding & Mansell Ltd Wisbech & London
on paper supplied by Spicers Ltd London
Text printed by Lowe & Brydone (Printers) Ltd London
on paper made by Grosvenor Chater Ltd London
and ruled by Tollit & Harvey Ltd London
Bound by the Leighton-Straker
Bookbinding Co Ltd London
FIFTH IMPRESSION 1960
© A. G. L. Hellyer 1955

FOREWORD

This book differs from many gardening encyclopaedias in that I have made no attempt to cover all the plants that are known in gardens. Instead I have chosen only those that are the best and most commonly grown in this country in the hope that this will enable many gardeners to acquire a better knowledge of more familiar and important plants. What has guided me throughout in its preparation is the belief that illustration is often more helpful than description when trying to familiarize gardeners with the varied and beautiful flowers that are now available to them. For this reason I have included one coloured picture of a typical species (kind) of each genus (group) I have mentioned and at least one illustration in line. In achieving this I have made use of the work of two artists, one living and the other long dead. Miss Cynthia Newsome-Taylor, who has prepared all the original paintings from which the coloured illustrations have been made, has worked in the closest association with me over a period of two years. Every painting has been done from living material. First she prepared hundreds of sketches in which she set down all the essential characteristics of the plant while it was still fresh, and then from these she made the final composite paintings in which all this miscellaneous material was assembled alphabetically. Both the artist and I have had a great deal of invaluable collaboration from other people, notably from Mr W. M. Campbell, the Curator of the Royal Botanic Gardens, Kew, from which most of the specimens were obtained.

For most of the line illustrations I went to a source which many people have forgotten, J. C. Loudon's *Encyclopaedia of Plants*, first published in 1829 and enlarged by supplements in 1841 and 1855. For this over 20,000 drawings were made by James de Carle Sowerby (1787-1871) the eldest son of James Sowerby (1757-1822) whose beautifully hand-coloured *Botany of British Plants* is still eagerly sought by collectors. Never before had so many species of garden plants been illustrated in a single volume. As Loudon stated in his preface of 1829, J. D. C. Sowerby, assisted by Mr David Don (librarian to the Linnean Society) and Messrs Loddiges, sought out the figures, dried specimens, or living plants, necessary for illustration, and made drawings of them on the blocks to be engraved, in that accurate and scientific manner and that appropriate taste for which his late father was so distinguished. One of the most expert wood-engravers of the day, Robert Branston, then cut the blocks. Their preparation occupied Sowerby for upwards of seven years. Loudon, an economical Scot, crammed his encyclopaedia almost indigestibly with information and Sowerby had to make his figures as small as possible so that from four to twenty could be fitted on to the same page as the corresponding text. For my book they have been enlarged about one and a half times, but such was the skill of both artist and engraver in preparing the minute originals that they actually gain by this enlargement.

Of course, in this book I have only used a very small proportion of the illustrations in Loudon's encyclopaedia. In making a selection I have taken those that seemed to me to be most typical of the genus they represent or to add most useful pictorial information to Miss Newsome-Taylor's paintings. They do not always depict the precise species I have described in my text, for here I have been guided rather by what is most readily available today or most

5

likely to be seen in gardens, but each of the plants illustrated is a desirable kind which is in cultivation, though not necessarily commercially popular.

The cultural notes I have prepared are inevitably very brief, but not more so than in most encyclopaedic books. For more detailed information the reader is referred to specialist works and this is particularly necessary with highly developed garden plants with rather complicated cultural requirements such as the rose, chrysanthemum and dahlia.

The nomenclature is botanical, but I have also included popular names wherever possible, including some which are not, perhaps, very familiar in this country but in my view might well be used. The American name Silk Tassel Bush for *Garrya elliptica* is an example, for it is most descriptive of the long, greenish-yellow winter catkins of that beautiful evergreen shrub. Most of the botanical names are those used in *Sanders' Encyclopaedia of Gardening* which I revised a few years ago, but sometimes I have kept to what I call the 'popular' botanical names to avoid confusion. Montbretia instead of Crocosmia, and Gloxinia instead of Sinningia are examples. I hope that even purists will agree that this is a sensible departure from strictly scientific nomenclature in what, after all, is meant to be a popular book with a particular appeal to the beginner and the unlearned.

For the benefit of readers who know the popular but not the botanical name of a particular plant I have included a comprehensive index of popular names with the appropriate cross-references. In this index I have also included some outdated botanical names which are still commonly used in nursery catalogues and are often the only reference to the plant which the gardener possesses. I hope that this system of arrangement will make the book easy to use by both the beginner and the expert.

In closing I want to thank a number of people for their help; Mr W. T. Stearn for detailed notes about Loudon and the Sowerbys from which I have quoted in this foreword; all the Assistant Curators at Kew for the generous way in which they have assisted me in finding suitable specimens, and Dr H. R. Fletcher, lately Director of the Royal Horticultural Society's gardens, Wisley, for making the great resources of that garden equally available. Without this help it would have been quite impossible to complete this book in so comparatively short a time.

Rowfant, 1955   A.G.L.HELLYER

THE PLATES

PLATE EIGHT
facing page 45

Dahlia (medium decorative) — Daphne Burkwoodii — Delphinium elatum (garden form) — Deutzia scabra — Dianthus plumarius (garden form) — Dianthus barbatus — Dicentra formosa — Dictamnus albus — Digitalis purpurea — Dimorphotheca aurantiaca — Dodecatheon Meadia — Doronicum plantagineum

PLATE NINE
facing page 48

Eccremocarpus scaber — Echinacea purpurea — Echinops bannaticus — Epimedium versicolor sulphureum — Eremurus himalaicus — Erica carnea — Erodium Manescavii — Eryngium planum — Erysimum Allionii — Escallonia langleyensis — Eschscholtzia californica — Euonymus europaeus — Felicia tenella

PLATE TEN
facing page 49

Forsythia intermedia spectabilis — Freesia refracta (garden form) — Fritillaria gracilis — Fuchsia 'Royal Purple' — Gaillardia aristata (garden form) — Galanthus nivalis — Galega officinalis — Gardenia jasminoides — Garrya elliptica — Gazania (garden forms) — Genista aethnensis — Gentiana septemfida — Geranium grandiflorum

PLATE ELEVEN
facing page 64

Gerbera Jamesonii — Geum coccineum (garden form) — Gladiolus (garden form) — Globularia cordifolia — Gloxinia (garden form) — Godetia amoena Schaminii — Gypsophila elegans — Hamamelis mollis — Helenium autumnale (garden form) — Helianthemum nummularium — Helianthus decapetalus multiflorus — Helichrysum bracteatum — Heliopsis scabra

PLATE TWELVE
facing page 65

Heliotropium arborescens — Helleborus niger — Hemerocallis (garden form) — Heuchera sanguinea (garden form) — Hibiscus syriacus — Hippeastrum (garden form) — Hosta lancifolia — Hoya carnosa — Hyacinthus orientalis — Hydrangea macrophylla Hortensia — Hypericum calycinum — Iberis sempervirens — Impatiens Sultanii

PLATE THIRTEEN
facing page 68

Incarvillea Delavayi — Ipomoea Leari — Iris siberica — Ixia hybrida — Jasminum nudiflorum — Kalanchoë Blossfeldiana — Kalmia latifolia — Kerria japonica — Kniphofia Uvaria nobilis — Laburnum vulgare — Lamium maculatum — Lantana Camara — Lapageria rosea

PLATE FOURTEEN
facing page 69

Lathyrus odoratus — Lavandula Spica — Lavatera trimestris — Leontopodium alpinum — Leptosyne maritima — Leucojum autumnale — Lewisia Tweedyi — Leycesteria formosa — Liatris spicata — Lilium candidum — Lilium speciosum rubrum — Limonium sinuatum

PLATE FIFTEEN
facing page 76

Linaria purpurea (garden form) — Linum narbonense — Lithospermum prostratum — Lobelia cardinalis — Lobelia tenuior — Lonicera Periclymenum — Lupinus polyphyllus (garden form) — Lychnis chalcedonica — Lysimachia vulgaris — Lythrum Salicaria — Magnolia Soulangeana — Mahonia Aquifolium — Malcolmia maritima

PLATE SIXTEEN
facing page 77

Malope trifida grandiflora — Malus Lemoinei — Matthiola incana — Meconopsis betonicifolia — Mesembryanthemum roseum — Mimulus luteus — Mirabilis Jalapa — Monarda didyma — Montbretia — Muscari botryoides — Myosotis dissitiflora — Narcissus incomparabilis — Narcissus poeticus

PLATE SEVENTEEN
facing page 80

Nemesia strumosa — Nemophila insignis — Nepeta Faassenii — Nerine Bowdenii — Nicotiana Sanderae — Nymphaea Marliacea — Oenothera fruticosa — Olearia Haastii — Omphalodes cappadocica — Ornithogalum umbellatum — Osmanthus Delavayi — Oxalis adenophylla — Paeonia officinalis

PLATE EIGHTEEN
facing page 81

Papaver orientale — Passiflora caerulea — Pelargonium zonale — Penstemon hybrida — Pernettya mucronata — Perovskia abrotanoides — Petunia hybrida — Phacelia campanularia — Philadelphus Lemoinei — Phlomis fruticosa — Phlox subulata — Phlox paniculata — Phygelius capensis

PLATE NINETEEN
facing page 96

Phyteuma Scheuchzeri — Platycodon grandiflorum — Plumbago capensis — Polemonium caeruleum — Polygonatum multiflorum — Polygonum affine — Potentilla fruticosa — Primula malacoides — Primula polyantha — Prunus serrulata — Pulmonaria officinalis — Pyracantha coccinea Lalandii

PLATE TWENTY
facing page 97

Ramonda Myconi — Reseda odorata — Rhododendron ponticum — Ranunculus asiaticus — Rhus typhina — Ribes sanguineum — Rodgersia pinnata — Romneya Coulteri — Rosa Moyesii — Rosa (Floribunda type) — Rosmarinus officinalis — Rudbeckia speciosa — Saintpaulia ionantha

PLATE TWENTY-ONE
facing page 100

Salpiglossis sinuata — Salvia splendens — Salvia patens — Sanguisorba obtusa — Santolina Chamaecyparissus — Saponaria Vaccaria — Saxifraga (mossy hybrid) — Saxifraga umbrosa — Saxifraga Burseriana — Scabiosa caucasica — Schizanthus hybridus — Scilla hispanica — Sedum spurium

PLATE TWENTY-TWO
facing page 101

Sempervivum calcareum — Senecio laxifolius — Sidalcea malvaeflora — Shortia uniflora grandiflora — Silene Schafta — Sisyrinchium angustifolium — Skimmia japonica — Solanum jasminoides album — Solidago canadensis — Spartium junceum — Spiraea Vanhouttei — Stachys lanata — Strelitzia Reginae

PLATE TWENTY-THREE
facing page 108

Streptocarpus hybridus — Symphoricarpos racemosus — Syringa vulgaris — Tagetes patula — Tamarix pentandra — Thalictrum dipterocarpum — Thymus Serpyllum — Tigridia Pavonia — Tradescantia virginiana — Trillium grandiflorum — Trollius europaeus — Tropaeolum majus

PLATE TWENTY-FOUR
facing page 109

Tulipa Gesneriana (garden form) — Venidium fastuosum — Verbascum Brousa — Verbena venosa — Veronica spicata — Viburnum Carlesii — Viburnum Opulus — Vinca minor — Viola tricolor — Weigela florida — Wisteria sinensis — Yucca filamentosa — Zinnia elegans

*Abutilon
venosum*

*Abutilon
integerrimum*

*Acacia armata
angustifolia*

*Acacia
verticillata*

ABUTILON *(Chinese Bellflower, Flowering Maple)*

All the important garden abutilons are shrubs, and all are either definitely tender, requiring protection in winter from all frost, or else are on the border-line of hardiness, thriving outdoors in sheltered places but liable to be destroyed by unusually severe weather. Some kinds are popular pot plants and some are much used for bedding out in summer, especially in the more elaborate schemes found in some public parks. All can be grown in any well-drained soil and can be increased by cuttings of firm shoots rooted in sandy soil in a close frame at practically any time, preferably in early autumn. Plants can be pruned to shape in spring.

The hardiest species is *A. vitifolium*, a big loose bush with grey-green leaves and soft mauve flowers in May. It makes a beautiful specimen in a warm sheltered place outdoors. Very striking is the sprawling *A. megapotamicum* with drooping red and yellow flowers in summer. It may be trained against a sunny wall outdoors or be grown as a cool greenhouse plant. The abutilons used for summer beddings are mostly hybrids with drooping bell shaped flowers and handsome lobed leaves. Very popular is *A. striatum Thompsonii*, with green leaves heavily mottled with yellow.

ACACIA *(Mimosa, Wattle)*

These are the shrubs or trees commonly known as mimosas though botanically that name belongs to quite a different plant. The common 'mimosa' of florist's shops with its fernlike leaves and fluffy yellow pompon flowers is *A. dealbata* which is just hardy enough to grow outdoors in some very mild parts of the country but must normally be treated as a greenhouse shrub. It will eventually make a fairly large tree if permitted to do so but can be kept far smaller by judicious pruning after flowering. There are a great many other species, mostly, like *A. dealbata*, natives of Australia where they are popularly known as wattles. The most popular as garden plants are *A. armata* with rounded phyllodes (flattened stems) instead of leaves and the typical yellow pompon flowers carried along the length of the branches; *A. decurrens* which is very like *A. dealbata* except that its foliage is green instead of grey; *A. Drummondii* with the yellow flowers crowded together in cylindrical spikes, and *A. longifolia* with loose spikes of yellow flowers and long narrow phyllodes.

All thrive in warm sunny places and rather light, well-drained soils. In greenhouses they may be grown in large pots but are really happier planted in a border. The most satisfactory way of increasing them is by seed sown in a warm greenhouse as soon as ripe (usually in late spring). Cuttings of half ripe shoots will root in summer in a close frame.

ACANTHUS *(Bear's Breech)*

Herbaceous plants with very handsome, thistle-like leaves and stiff, erect spikes of broadly tube shaped flowers which are

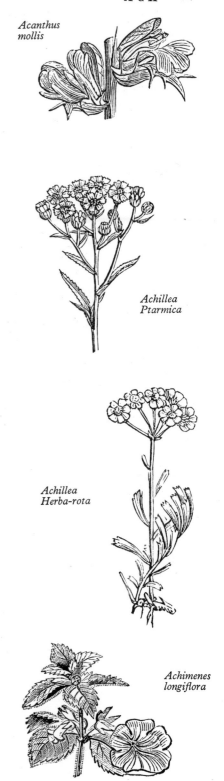

Acanthus
mollis

Achillea
Ptarmica

Achillea
Herba-rota

Achimenes
longiflora

usually dull rose or purple and white. The effect is subdued but distinctive and the cut flower stems keep their colour for a long time and make good winter decorations. All flower in summer. These attractive plants are not in the least fussy about soil and will thrive in full sun or partial shade. They can be increased from seed sown in a frame in spring but usually sufficient plants for all requirements can be obtained by carefully dividing old roots in spring. The two best species are *A. mollis* with 3-foot flower spikes and broad lobed leaves, and *A. spinosus*, similar in height, but with much more deeply and finely cut leaves, which are spiny.

ACHILLEA *(Milfoil, Yarrow)*

A big family of hardy perennials very easily grown in practically any kind of soil and reasonably open situation. They can be increased by dividing the roots in spring or autumn and can also be raised from seed sown in a frame or greenhouse in spring.

Achilleas may be roughly divided into two groups, the taller kinds, most suitable for herbaceous borders, and the dwarf and spreading kinds for rock gardens or walls. Of the former one of the best is *Achillea filipendulina* (sometimes known as *A. Eupatorium*). Four or five feet tall, it produces in July and August, nearly flat, plate-like heads of yellow flowers. Not unlike this but much smaller is *A. taygetea* with finely divided silvery leaves and lemon yellow flower heads on 2-foot stems in June and July. Another good border plant is *A. Ptarmica*, best known in its double flowered form, The Pearl, a fine plant for cutting. About 2 feet high, it bears small, almost globular pure white flowers, in small clusters, from June to August.

A fourth herbaceous species is *A. millefolium* in either of its brightly carmine coloured varieties, *Kelwayi* or Cerise Queen.

Perhaps the best of the dwarf kinds is the hybrid King Edward VII, with small heads of sulphur yellow flowers produced continuously from June to September. *A. tomentosa* is a little coarser and bright yellow rather than sulphur. A refined hybrid of this, with grey leaves and pale yellow flowers, is *A. Lewisii*. Others worth consideration are *A. argentea* and *A. Clavennae*, two similar plants, with white flowers and silvery leaves, and *A. ageratifolia*, also white and silver but more dwarf in habit.

ACHIMENES *(Hot Water Plant)*

These showy greenhouse plants are sometimes known as hot water plants because Victorian gardeners thought that they liked to be watered with hot water. They produce small tubers and it is by new tubers produced as offshoots from the old ones that they can most readily be propagated. Seed may be used but needs a temperature of around 70° to germinate it. Cuttings of the firm young growths may be taken in spring, but a fairly high temperature is needed to ensure root formation.

Tubers are started into growth in sandy soil in shallow seed boxes from January to May. They should be just covered with similar soil and made slightly moist, and afterwards placed in a

*Achimenes
grandiflora*

*Aconitum
Fischeri*

*Aconitum
Cammarum*

*Aethionema
saxatile*

temperature of 60–65°. When the young shoots are an inch or so high, the tubers should be transferred to pots in John Innes compost. They may be grown either singly in 3½ or 4–inch pots or several together in larger pots, and as they are trailing in habit, they may be placed in baskets suspended from the greenhouse roof or in their pots at the edge of the greenhouse staging. They will need plenty of water while growing and flowering, which they will do from June to September if batches of tubers are started successively. After flowering, watering must be decreased until growth dies right down, when the tubers can be shaken out and stored in a dry, frost-proof place until it is time to start them once more.

All the achimenes grown in gardens to-day are unnamed hybrids in a variety of rich colours including blue, purple and red.

ACONITUM *(Monkshood, Aconite, but not the Winter Aconite which is Eranthis Hyemalis)*

Hardy herbaceous perennials, related to the delphiniums and having a faint resemblance to them when bearing their erect spikes of mainly blue or purple flowers. The individual flowers, however, are hooded and not open as in the delphinium. All like cool, moist soils and thrive in the edges of woods or on shady borders. They can be increased by division of their roots in spring or autumn and can also be raised from seed sown in a greenhouse or frame in the spring.

One of the best species is *A. Napellus* an uncommon British wild plant, well worth a place in the garden. Its 3–foot spikes of bluish-purple flowers are produced in June and July. It has several useful varieties including Sparke's variety a very deep purple. *A. Cammarum bicolor* is white edged with blue. Other worthwhile species are *A. Fischeri*, a good medium blue which flowers in September, and *A. Wilsoni*, said to be a form of *A. Carmichaelii*, a taller plant.

All are poisonous and all resent being transplanted and may take some little time to recover.

AETHIONEMA *(Stone Cress)*

These are tiny shrubs or half-woody plants for the rock garden or dry wall. They have narrow leaves closely set all along the stems which are terminated by small heads of pink flowers like those of a very neat candytuft. They love sun and good drainage and, though usually seen as quite small plants, perhaps 1 foot high and as much through, will double those dimensions under favourable conditions. All can be most readily raised from seed sown in a frame or unheated greenhouse in spring, but cuttings of firm young shoots will also root readily in sandy soil in a close frame or propagating box in July.

The best kinds are *A. grandiflorum*, light rose pink, *A. pulchellum*, usually rather paler in colour, and *A. warleyense* (Warley Rose), neater and bushier in habit than either of the foregoing and brighter in colour.

12

AGAPANTHUS (*African Lily*)

The popular African lily, most familiar as a pot or tub plant, bears bright blue, lily-like flowers all the summer. This is *A. umbellatus* which is not quite hardy except in the very mildest parts of Britain, and must, therefore, be given greenhouse protection from October to May. However, a fine form of this plant, named *Mooreanus*, not only has darker blue flowers, but is considerably hardier and can be grown in the open in many parts of the country.

All kinds can be increased by division of the roots in March or by seeds sown in spring in a greenhouse or frame. Under glass very little water should be given in winter, when the plants may be allowed to become almost completely dormant. Outdoors the agapanthus should be given a sunny, well-drained position and watered well in summer if dry.

*Agapanthus
umbellatus*

AGERATUM (*Floss Flower*)

A very attractive little plant with fluffy heads of soft blue flowers. A favourite bedding plant for use as a groundwork beneath taller plants or as an edging, it is almost always treated as a half-hardy annual though it is a perennial and can be kept from year to year provided it is protected from frost. The easiest way of growing ageratum, however, is to sow seed thinly in a warm greenhouse in February or March, prick off the seedlings 1½ inch apart and then harden them off in a frame ready for planting out about 6 inches apart in May when the spring bedding has been cleared away. Ageratum will grow in full sun or partial shade and is not fussy about soil.

*Ageratum
Houstonianum*

ALLIUM (*Onion, Garlic*)

There are several onion species sufficiently decorative in flower to be worth a place in the flower garden. The most familiar is *Allium Moly*, a cheerful plant with heads of buttercup yellow flowers carried on stiff, foot high stems in May. It will grow anywhere, indeed it can become a bit of a weed. Less invasive and far more imposing is *A. Rosenbachianum* with great, globular heads of reddish purple flowers on 4-foot stems in May. *A. Ostrowskianum* has equally large and spherical heads of bloom, much paler in colour and carried on rather stumpy stems. *A. albo-pilosum* has lilac flowers and is otherwise similar to the last, but completely different is *A. descendens* with quite small, compact, egg shaped heads of deep maroon flowers produced in July at the tips of slender stems. *A. pulchellum* is a dainty species with heads of lilac flowers. All can be grown in almost any kind of soil provided they have plenty of sun. They are best increased by dividing the clusters of bulbs in late summer.

*Allium
descendens*

ALSTROEMERIA (*Peruvian Lily*)

Best known of the Peruvian lilies is *A. aurantiaca*, which has small orange flowers, flecked or speckled with black, very freely produced in July and August on 3-foot stems. Its white, ropy

*Allium
Moly*

Alstroemeria
Pelegrina

Alstroemeria
psittacina

Althaea
rosea

Alyssum
montanum

roots are sometimes slow to recover after being moved, but once established they spread rapidly. The flowers last well when cut and are much grown for market. Choicer but more difficult is *A. Ligtu*, with large heads of pink flowers in July. Hybrids have been raised from this in many shades of pink, salmon, apricot and flame and these are the best of all to grow. They are very readily raised from seed sown either as soon as ripe in late summer, or in spring, but the seedlings must be handled with care if they are to be established successfully. I find it best to sow thinly in rather deep seed boxes and leave the seedlings undisturbed the first year. In March the fleshy, almost transparent roots can be carefully shaken out and planted 5 inches deep and 3 to 4 feet apart in fairly rich well-drained soil, in a sunny position. They may do little the first year but will spread underground and should come up with increasing vigour each succeeding spring.

A. aurantiaca can be increased from seed, but it is easier to lift and divide the roots in spring, replanting them at least 5 inches deep.

ALTHAEA *(Hollyhock)*

The hollyhock is so familiar that it needs no introduction. There are few better tall plants for the back of the border and none that will thrive better in poor soil, though they will also respond to more generous culture, particularly the fine double-flowered forms. Though a short-lived perennial like the lupin, it is often more convenient to treat the hollyhock as a biennial, sowing seed outdoors in May to flower the following year. Seedlings should be removed to a nursery bed in July and planted about 6 inches apart to grow into sturdy plants ready for removal in October to their flowering quarters. There are also strains which can be treated as annuals, being sown in a greenhouse in February, hardened off and planted out in May, to flower in summer. Specially desirable forms of the ordinary hollyhock can be increased by root cuttings inserted in sandy soil in winter, thus keeping them true to type.

ALYSSUM *(Madwort, Gold Dust)*

Two principal kinds of alyssum are grown in gardens, one an annual and the other a perennial. The annual is *A. maritimum*, often known as sweet alyssum because of the honey-like fragrance of its clusters of small white or purple flowers. A dwarf plant very suitable for carpeting beneath taller plants or for use as an edging, it will flower for weeks on end, in early summer if sown in September or March, and in later summer if sown in April or May. Seed should be sown thinly where the plants are to flower and the seedlings thinned to 6 inches apart.

The common perennial species is *A. saxatile*, often known as gold dust because of the abundance of its small golden yellow flowers. A taller and bushier plant than the annual alyssum, with coarser, greyish leaves, it is most suitable for rock gardens or dry walls. It is readily raised from seed which may be sown in a greenhouse or frame in March or outdoors in April or May,

Amaryllis
Belladonna

Amelanchier
vulgaris

Amelanchier
oblongifolia

Anchusa
capensis

to flower the following year. The variety *citrinum* has lemon yellow flowers, and another named *flore pleno*, with double flowers, is best increased by cuttings struck in a close frame in spring or early summer.

Smaller, neater but less showy are *A. spinosum* with white flowers in early summer and *A. montanum* with yellow flowers. They should be grown in the same way as *A. saxatile*. All like sunny places and well-drained soils but are not difficult.

AMARYLLIS *(Belladonna Lily, Jersey Lily)*

Amaryllis Belladonna is a choice plant which produces its intensely fragrant, rose pink, trumpet shaped flowers in the autumn before the leaves appear. Hardy in a sunny sheltered position, it does very well in most of the southern counties, particularly if planted near the foot of a wall facing south. The bulbs should be planted 4 or 5 inches deep in early autumn and thereafter should be left undisturbed for as long as possible as they re-establish themselves rather slowly. Though it likes light, well-drained soils, it does not appreciate being starved and can be fed from time to time with top dressings of well rotted manure or compost. It can be increased by splitting up the bulb clusters at planting time.

AMELANCHIER *(Snowy Mespilus)*

These are graceful flowering trees of small to medium size, which deserve to be better known. Their small but abundant white flowers are produced in April and May and in the autumn their dying foliage turns a brilliant crimson. The best species, *A. canadensis*, may eventually reach a height of about 25 feet. *A. oblongifolia*, which is very similar, rather smaller but still a tree. By contrast *A. ovalis* (syn. *A. vulgaris*,), seldom exceeds 8 feet in height and is a shrub rather than a tree. None of these requires pruning. They can be increased rather slowly by seed sown in greenhouse or frame in spring, but nurserymen, to save time, often bud or graft them on to mountain ash. Some kinds produce suckers freely and these can be dug up in autumn and planted separately. November is the best planting month. Amelanchiers are not particular about soil.

ANCHUSA *(Alkanet)*

The most popular of the alkanets, *Anchusa italica*, a hardy perennial, might be described as a very stiff forget-me-not on a vastly increased scale. It grows 4 or 5 feet in height and the individual, bright blue flowers, produced in June, may be an inch in diameter. The garden varieties of this fine plant, differ mainly in the precise shade of their blue. Opal is a light blue, whereas Morning Glory and Dropmore are a deeper blue. All can be increased by root cuttings inserted in winter in sandy soil or by careful division of the roots in March. Seed sown in a frame in March or outdoors in May also germinates readily but there may be some slight variation in the colour of the flowers produced by the seedlings. The perennial alkanets dislike excessively damp soil in

15

*Androsace
Chamaejasme*

*Androsace
lanuginosa*

*Anemone
coronaria*

*Anemone
apennina*

winter and may prove short lived under such conditions.

Another useful species is *A. capensis*, a biennial about 18 inches high with smaller blue flowers. Seed should be sown out-doors in May to produce plants to flower the following year.

ANDROSACE *(Rock Jasmine)*

The androsaces have no resemblance to or connexion with the climbing jasmines. They are tussock-forming or trailing plants suitable for rock gardens and dry walls. Some come from high altitudes and prove difficult in cultivation, only thriving when given the sharpest possible drainage in soil containing an abundant quantity of stone chippings. *A. Chamaejasme, A. helvetica* and *A. imbricata* belong to this class. By contrast there are quite easy androsaces such as *A. lanuginosa* and *A. sarmentosa*, which can be grown in any ordinary soil provided it is reasonably well drained. Both have grey-green leaves and small, round pink flowers, but whereas *A. sarmentosa* is compact, forms rosettes and flowers in May, June, *A. lanuginosa* is more trailing and flowers several weeks later. All these can be increased by careful division in spring or by seed sown in spring in very sandy compost in greenhouse or frame.

ANEMONE *(Windflower)*

There are a great many anemones differing so much from one another in appearance that it may seem strange that they should all be grouped in one genus. From the garden standpoint one may broadly distinguish three principal groups; the dwarf, woodland windflowers with small, fragile flowers; the poppy anemones, all sun lovers and excellent for cutting, with cup shaped flowers in brilliant colours and stems a foot to 18 inches in length; and the herbaceous border anemones 2 to 4 feet in height, all good perennials, with a tendency to ramble.

The most familiar woodland kind is the native *A. nemorosa*, a common plant in woods, very pretty with its dainty white flowers on slender stems, but not worth cultivation except in the wild garden. It has, however, a number of good varieties of which *Robinsoniana* with pale blue flowers, is worth using as a carpeting plant beneath shrubs. More popular and more showy are *A. apennina* and *A. blanda*, very similar plants making rapidly spreading clumps of deeply cut, almost ferny leaves from which spring, in March and April, a profusion of delightful blue flowers. There are also white and pink coloured forms but not so beautiful as the common blue. All these will spread rapidly given a reasonably good, leafy soil and a position sheltered from hot sunshine but not too densely shady. They can be propagated by division immediately after flowering.

The poppy anemones are derived from *A. coronaria*, but *A. fulgens*, with scarlet flowers, is a very similar plant which should be grown in the same way. They like a sunny place in fairly good, well drained, but firm soil. Often planted in straight rows in large beds specially for cutting, they may also be grown in the rock garden or towards the front of the herbaceous border. They

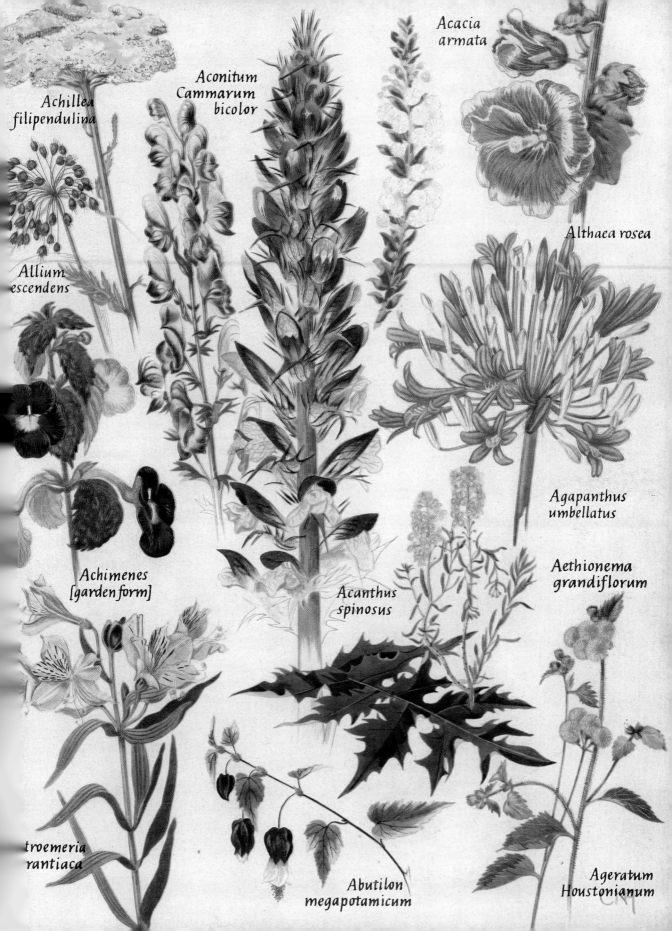

Achillea
filipendulina

Aconitum
Cammarum
bicolor

Acacia
armata

Allium
escendens

Althaea rosea

Achimenes
[garden form]

Acanthus
spinosus

Agapanthus
umbellatus

Aethionema
grandiflorum

troemeria
rantiaca

Abutilon
megapotamicum

Ageratum
Houstonianum

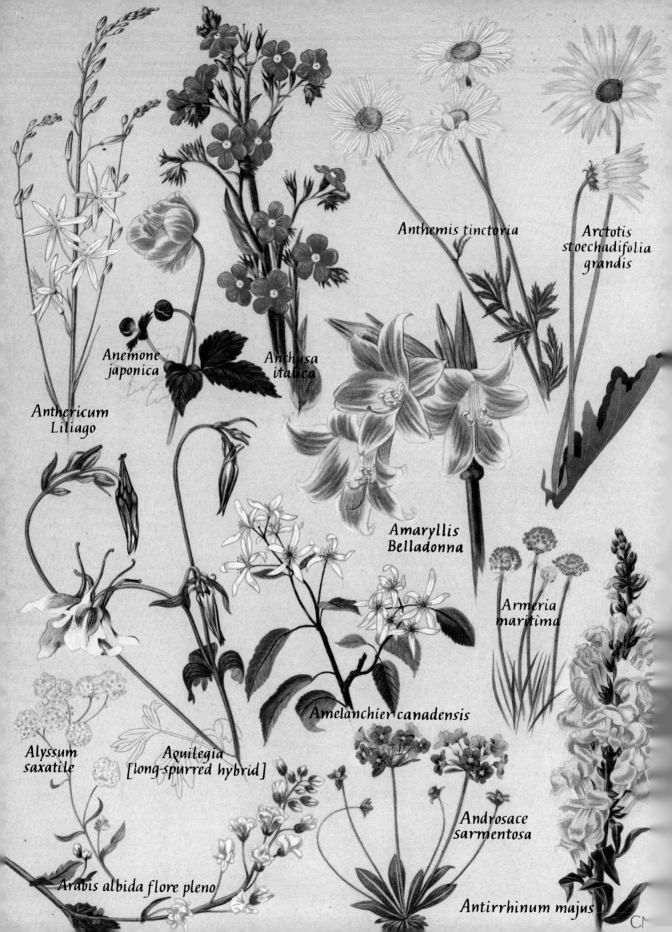

Anthemis tinctoria

Arctotis
stoechadifolia
grandis

Anemone
japonica

Anchusa
italica

Anthericum
Liliago

Amaryllis
Belladonna

Armeria
maritima

Amelanchier canadensis

Alyssum
saxatile

Aquilegia
[long-spurred hybrid]

Androsace
sarmentosa

Arabis albida flore pleno

Antirrhinum majus

make quite sizeable tubers which may be lifted in late summer and stored in a dry, frost-proof place until the following February or March. This is advisable in very cold or damp places. Propagation is either by dividing the clusters of tubers when they are lifted or by sowing seed outdoors in late May or early June. There are a number of fine strains of the poppy anemone of which St Brigid with double flowers in various shades from purple to scarlet and Du Caen with single flowers in similar colours are the best.

The most familiar herbaceous species is *A. japonica* in its white and pink flowered forms, flowering in August and September. The flowers are 2 to 3 inches across, saucer shaped and carried well above the vine-like leaves. Once established it is capable of taking complete charge of quite a lot of ground, but it dislikes root disturbance and is sometimes slow to start. Roots can be divided or transplanted in spring.

Anemone japonica

ANTHEMIS *(Chamomile, Golden Marguerite)*

The most useful anthemis for the garden is the so-called golden marguerite, *A. tinctoria*, a first rate border plant and a very useful cut flower. It makes a big, bushy plant 2 or 3 feet in height and even more through, with deeply cut, rather ferny leaves and masses of bright yellow daisy flowers carried on long stems during July and August. The varieties differ mainly in the size and precise shade of their flowers. All should be planted in a sunny place in March or April and should not be disturbed in autumn. Propagate by cuttings of firm young shoots inserted during spring or early summer in sandy soil in a frame.

Anthemis montana

ANTHERICUM *(St Bernard's Lily)*

The true St Bernard's Lily, *Anthericum Liliago*, is an attractive hardy herbaceous plant making neat clumps of narrow grassy foliage from which spring in June, foot high stems carrying white, lily like flowers. Nearly allied is the St Bruno's Lily, which used to be known as *A. Liliastrum* (and still is in most gardens) but has now been renamed *Paradisea Liliastrum*. It is very similar to the St Bernard's Lily but about twice as tall. Both have garden varieties, distinguished by such names as 'major' and 'grandiflorum', which have larger flowers. All grow in any ordinary soil and open place and are readily increased by dividing the roots in spring.

Anthericum ramosum

ANTIRRHINUM *(Snapdragon)*

Though almost always grown as a half hardy annual, the antirrhinum is, in fact, a nearly hardy perennial. In warm, sheltered places, particularly in poor and sharply drained soil, plants several years old are often to be seen. Nevertheless, the most satisfactory method of growing antirrhinums is to sow seed each January or February in a warm greenhouse or frame, prick out the seedlings as soon as they can be handled and then harden off in a frame for planting outdoors in May.

Antirrhinums like sunshine and good drainage but in very

Antirrhinum majus

*Aquilegia
alpina*

*Aquilegia
glauca*

*Arctotis
acaulis*

*Arctotis
stoechadifolia*

hot, dry places are apt to suffer badly from rust disease. This is far less likely to be troublesome where the climate is cool and rather damp. Rust resistant varieties are available and should be used where the disease is prevalent.

Antirrhinums are available in a wide range of colours including yellow, apricot, orange, pink, scarlet and crimson, and in varying heights ranging from 'Tom Thumb' varieties about 1 foot high, to 'Tall' varieties, 3 feet high. All are useful for filling beds and borders with a mass of colour.

AQUILEGIA *(Columbine)*

The long-spurred columbines with their very graceful flowers, carried like butterflies on stiff but slender stems are among the best loved flowers of early summer. The colours are mostly delicate shades of yellow, pink, lavender, blue and mauve but there are also quite bright shades of red and crimson. All can be raised from seed sown outdoors in May or early June. Selected colour forms may be increased by careful division of the roots in March or April. Aquilegias will thrive equally well in full sunshine or in light shade and in any soil but are apt to be short lived in heavy and wet clay soils. There are smaller species which are delightful rock garden plants. Among the best are *A. caerulea*, pale blue and white flowers on 15 to 18-inch stems, and *A. glandulosa*, lilac blue and white flowers on foot high stems. Both are spring flowering. *Aquilegia alpina* with blue flowers borne on 6 to 18-inch stems is more difficult.

ARABIS *(Rock Cress)*

A grand trailing plant that will soon cover a square yard or more of wall or rock garden with its carpets of grey-green leaves which completely disappear in April beneath the smother of its pure white flowers. *Arabis albida* has single flowers whereas in *A. albida flore pleno* each bloom is double, like a little white pompon. For some reason the double form, which is the better plant, has become quite scarce. Both will grow easily in any sunny position and any soil. They are seen to best advantage if planted at the top of a wall to cascade down its face. They can be increased by cuttings of young shoots taken a few weeks after flowering, inserted in sandy soil in a frame. The single arabis can also be raised from seed sown in a frame in March or outdoors in May.

ARCTOTIS

These South African half-hardy annuals are attractive plants for a sunny position. All are large summer-flowering daisies, some with long slender stems, some stemless, and many with stems of intermediate length. *Arctotis stoechadifolia grandis* is most unusual in colour, a silvery white with pale blue reverse and these elegant flowers are carried on long slender stems. There are also hybrids with shorter and stouter stems and large flowers in various shades of orange, red, yellow and wine, often with a darker central zone of colour. All can be raised from seed sown in February or March in warmth under glass, the seedlings being pricked off at least 2 inches apart and hardened off for planting out 1 foot apart in late May where they are to flower.

ARMERIA *(Thrift)*

The smaller thrifts, such as our native *Armeria maritima*, with its globular heads of pink or rose flowers on 6-inch stems, and the stemless and paler pink *A. caespitosa*, are excellent for the rock garden or dry wall. The taller kinds, of which *A. pseudo-armeria* (*cephalotes*) and its improved variety 'Bees Ruby' are the best, can also be grown in the rock garden but are really more at home towards the front of the herbaceous border. All flower in May or June. The small kinds make tussocks of rather narrow, grassy leaves, but *A. pseudo-armeria* has rather broader, heavier leaves. They like sunny places and well-drained soils and will grow in the poorest of sandy soils. They can be increased by careful division of the roots in spring or autumn.

ARTEMISIA *(Wormwood, Southernwood)*

It must be confessed that most artemisias are too coarse or unattractive to be of much use in the garden. Nevertheless there are some excellent silver-leaved plants for the front of the herbaceous border. *A. gnaphalodes* is typical of these, a hardy perennial 2 feet high, with inconspicuous flowers but very handsome grey-white leaves. *A. frigida* is even more decorative because its silvery leaves are deeply and finely divided. *A. argentea*, *A. Ludoviciana* and *A. Stelleriana* are three more of the same persuasion but their names tend to be confused and it is desirable to see them in growth before purchasing them. A taller plant with green leaves and fine sprays of small cream coloured flowers in August is *A. lactiflora*, a fine plant for the middle or back of the herbaceous border and one that does not mind a certain amount of shade. The silver-leaved kinds prefer sun and are seen to best advantage in rather poor soils. All these can be increased by division, in the spring. There are, in addition, some sub-shrubby kinds of which the Southernwood or Old Man, *A. Abrotanum* is the most familiar example, which cannot be divided but can be increased by cuttings of firm young shoots inserted in sandy soil in a frame in early summer. The Southernwood makes a big bush 4 or 5 feet in height and as much through, with finely divided, fragrant grey-green leaves. Another sub-shrubby kind is the true Wormwood, *A. Absinthium*, with silky white leaves.

ARUM

The familiar white arum lily of florists' shops, once known botanically as arum or richardia, is now *Zantedeschia aethiopica*. It is a greenhouse plant which can only be grown outdoors in a few of the mildest parts of the country, as in Cornwall or the Channel Islands. The 'flowers' are, in fact, spathes surrounding a central yellow spadix which carries the true flowers.

All arums have fleshy roots and can be increased by careful division of these roots in August or early September. This is

Armeria maritima

Armeria pseudo-armeria

Artemisia spicata

Arum (Zantedeschia aethiopica)

19

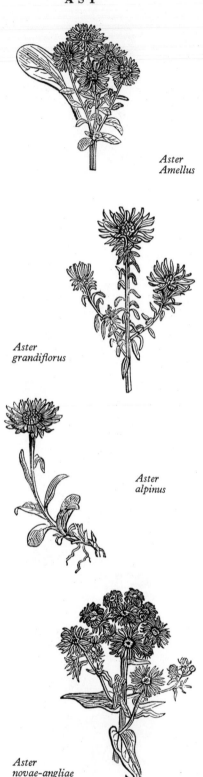

Aster
Amellus

Aster
grandiflorus

Aster
alpinus

Aster
novae-angliae

also the time to pot or re-pot the plants. Single roots may be placed in 6 or 7–inch pots or two or three roots can be accommodated in a 10–inch pot. The crown of the root should be just at soil level. John Innes compost will suit these plants well but it may be an advantage to add just a little well-rotted stable or cow manure, particularly if the loam is not very rich. After potting, the arums should be kept quite cool in a frame or unheated greenhouse for a month, and watered moderately, but as growth increases, more water can be given and the temperature can be gradually increased if early flowers are required. However, if flowers are not needed until the normal time in May, no heat need be used except to exclude frost. In June the plants can be knocked out of their pots and planted outdoors without further root disturbance but they should not be allowed to get dry at any time for they like abundant moisture while in growth.

ASTER *(Michaelmas Daisy)*

This is a family in which botanical and popular names are muddled. The plants which the botanist calls aster are all herbaceous perennials and the most familiar of them are the michaelmas daisies. The half-hardy annuals which are popularly known as 'asters' in gardens, are called callistephus. However, for simplicity I am treating them all together here.

The perennial asters are all very hardy and will thrive in practically any soil and situation. The michaelmas daisies may be considered in three groups; those with smooth leaves derived from *Aster novi-belgii*, the downy-leaved varieties derived from *A. novae-angliae*, and the much more bushy and branching varieties derived from *A. Amellus* and *A. Frikartii*. These are usually known simply as 'Amellus varieties'. They differ from the others not only in their habit but also in their rather earlier flowering season (they are at their best in August and early September) and by their dislike of being transplanted at any time except the spring. Most are between 2 and 3 feet in height and have large, single flowers in shades of blue, lilac or mauve.

The *novae-angliae* varieties all tend to close their flowers at night, which is a disadvantage. They are rather tall plants, increasing rapidly in size, and their flowers are either a deep rose or else purple. One of the best known is Barr's Pink.

The most highly developed race of michaelmas daisies has been derived from *A. novi-belgii*. Heights range from about a foot to at least 6 feet, colours from white and palest pink or mauve to deepest rose, carmine and purple. There are varieties with semi-double flowers as well as singles and the flowering season is September and October.

All these asters, and also such species as *A. ericoides* with small white flowers, *A. cordifolius* with arching sprays of mauve flowers, and the alpine species *A. alpinus*, *A. Farreri* and *A. sub-caeruleus*, can be readily increased by division of the roots in autumn or spring (but only spring for *A. Amellus* and its varieties).

The annual asters derived from *Callistephus chinensis* are

totally different plants. They have much larger flowers borne singly on stems seldom above 2 feet in length. There are fully double as well as single flowered varieties and the doubles vary greatly in form, some having narrow curled petals building up a rather shaggy looking bloom and others being broader, stiffer and more formal in character. The ostrich plume asters are an example of the shaggy type, whereas the comets have straight petals. Colours include blue, mauve, pink, red and white.

All these can be raised from seed sown in a greenhouse or frame in March or April or outdoors in early May. Seedlings raised under glass must be pricked off and then hardened off for planting outdoors in May. All flower in late summer and early autumn. They are ideal for late bedding and the long stemmed varieties make good cut flowers.

ASTILBE (False Goatsbeard)

There is some confusion between the astilbes and the spiraeas. The latter are mainly shrubs whereas the astilbes are herbaceous perennials bearing graceful plumes of flowers. Plants for moist places, they will stand a certain amount of shade as well. They are, perhaps, happiest near the water side but can also be grown in the ordinary border provided the soil does not dry out too severely. Though perfectly hardy and quite happy if left out of doors all the year, they also make good pot plants for the unheated or slightly heated greenhouse or conservatory. For this strong roots should be lifted in October or November, placed in pots that will contain their roots comfortably and, after a month or so in a frame, removed to the greenhouse. No attempt should be made to force them unduly and they must be kept well watered throughout the time that they are growing and flowering.

There are many garden varieties, from $1\frac{1}{2}$ to 5 feet high, ranging in colour from white and palest pink to a deep wine red. All flower in June or early July but may be had in flower at least two months earlier under glass. Propagation is by careful division of the clumps in spring or autumn.

AUBRIETA (Coloured Rock Cress)

This will soon make fine sheets and curtains of its neat bright green leaves which will be completely covered in April and May by the mauve, purple, pink or crimson flowers. Aubrietas thrive in chalky soils but will grow anywhere if the drainage is good and there are stones to ramble over or walls to hang down. They can be raised from seed sown in spring in a frame, or in early summer outdoors. Seedlings always vary a little in colour and selected forms must be propagated by cuttings taken in late June or early July. It is a good plan to trim over the plants lightly with scissors or shears after flowering. The first young shoots that appear after this trimming make the best cuttings. They should be inserted in sandy soil in a frame.

AZALEA

Botanically all azaleas are rhododendrons but from the garden standpoint it is convenient to consider them separately. They

21

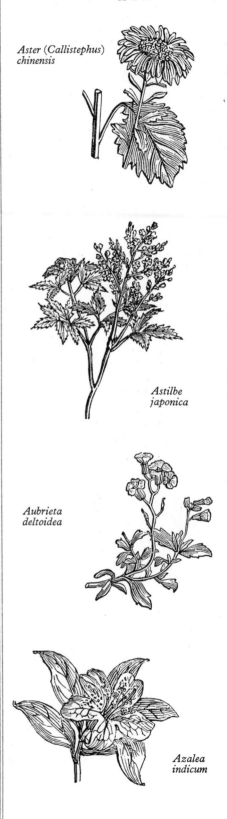

Aster (Callistephus) chinensis

Astilbe japonica

Aubrieta deltoidea

Azalea indicum

*Azalea
luteum*

*Azalea
obtusa*

*Begonia
nitida*

*Begonia
Evansiana*

may be divided into two main groups, the evergreen azaleas, compact bushes with neat foliage and comparatively small, but often very brilliantly coloured flowers, and the deciduous azaleas which make larger and looser bushes with flowers which are also much bigger individually though they do not, on that account, necessarily make a better display.

Very popular examples of the evergreen azaleas are the Kurume varieties. These are comparatively dwarf plants though they may eventually grow into quite big bushes 4 or 5 feet high and even more through. They are related to the vividly magenta flowered *Azalea obtusum amoenum* but are generally in colours a little less barbaric and difficult to associate. All flower in late April or early May and are grand for a large rock garden, for the front of shrub borders or for fairly open places in woodland. They like cool soils, well supplied with humus and they dislike lime. The varieties of *A. indica*, which have fine double flowers are a little tender and are grown as greenhouse plants.

The deciduous azaleas succeed very well in full sun but also thrive in thin woodland. They make big bushes 6 to 8 feet high and as much through and have flowers in many bright colours, particularly shades of yellow, apricot, orange, flame, pink, rose and crimson. There are several different races distinguished by such names as Mollis hybrids, Ghent hybrids, etc. There is also a beautiful race with semi-double or 'hose-in-hose' flowers known as *rustica flore pleno*. All are at their best in the latter half of April and throughout May.

All single-flowered azaleas can be increased from seed sown very thinly in spring and barely covered with fine soil containing plenty of peat and sand. Selected varieties and doubles must be propagated by cuttings prepared from firm young shoots in July and rooted in sandy peat in a close frame, preferably with a little bottom heat.

BEGONIA

Begonias are popular greenhouse plants and some can also be used for bedding out displays in summer, though all are too tender to survive frost. There are many different kinds, but for ordinary purposes it will be sufficient to consider five principal types. There are the summer-flowering tuberous rooted kinds, mostly with very large double blooms, though there are also single-flowered varieties; the nearly allied pendulous begonias also with tuberous roots; the small-flowered summer begonias, readily raised from seed and, for that reason, often treated as half-hardy annuals; the small-flowered winter flowering begonias of which the famous variety Gloire de Lorraine is the type; and the Rex begonias which are grown for the beauty of their large, multi-coloured leaves.

Taking these in order, both the large-flowered, tuberous-rooted and the smaller-flowered pendulous varieties may be stored in winter in some dry peat or sand in a frost proof place, such as a cupboard indoors. In January, February or March, according to the artificial heat available, the tubers are laid in seed boxes filled with damp peat or leaf mould and placed in a temperature of around 60°. Leaves will soon appear and then the tubers can be potted singly in 4–, 5– or 6– inch pots.

The small-flowered summer begonias, with pink, red or white flowers, popular for bedding, are derived from *B. semperflorens*, and are usually raised from seed sown in February or March in a temperature of 60° to 65°. The seedlings are pricked out into small pots or fairly deep seed boxes in which they can be hardened off for planting outdoors in early June. They will grow and flower perfectly well in full sun provided plenty of peat, leaf mould or old compost is first mixed with the soil to hold moisture. After flowering the plants are usually thrown away.

Winter flowering begonias of the Gloire de Lorraine type with their loose sprays of small pink or white flowers, are very pretty plants to have around Christmas, but they need temperatures of about 65° to 70° to be flowered successfully. They are usually raised from cuttings of firm, young basal shoots rooted in a propagating frame, with bottom heat, from January to March.

The Rex begonias also need warmth throughout the winter as they are tender and have no resting season. Otherwise their treatment is much the same as for the tuberous rooted begonias and they will certainly survive in lower temperatures than the winter flowering begonias.

BELLIS (Daisy)

The common daisy of lawns and meadows (*Bellis perennis*) has given rise to a number of varieties with larger double flowers, useful plants for spring displays, particularly beneath taller plants such as tulips. Some are white, some pink and some red, and they also differ in the size of their flowers. They are perennials and can be kept from year to year but it is usual to treat them as biennials, sowing the seed outdoors each year in May, or early June, pricking the seedlings out about 6 inches apart in a nursery bed in July, and transferring them to their flowering quarters in September or October. They are then thrown away after flowering. The choice varieties, of which the most notable is the small pink Dresden China, should be increased by division in spring.

BERBERIS (Barberry)

The barberries are shrubs, some evergreen and some deciduous, producing yellow or orange flowers some time in spring or early summer, followed by berries, usually deep purple or black in the evergreens and red in the deciduous kinds. Generally it is the flowers which make the best display in the evergreens and the berries which are the principal attraction in the deciduous species. All are very hardy, not fussy about soil, preferring fairly sunny and open places. They do not need pruning. Most are quite easy to transplant in autumn or early spring, but one or two, notably *Berberis Darwinii*, are a little difficult as they resent root disturbance. It is best to raise this fine species in pots so that it

Begonia semperflorens

Begonia coccinea

Begonia Meyeri

Berberis Darwinii

23

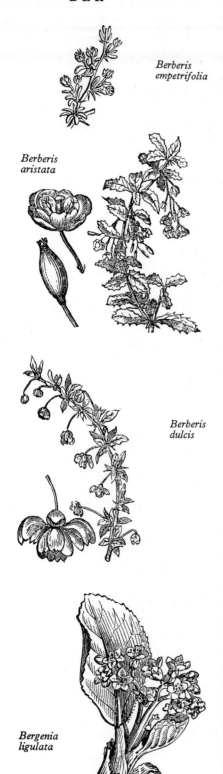

Berberis
empetrifolia

Berberis
aristata

Berberis
dulcis

Bergenia
ligulata

can be planted with its roots more or less intact. Propagation is very easily effected by sowing seed in pots or boxes, or direct in the open ground in March. Seedlings usually begin to flower and fruit in about their third or fourth year. Alternatively cuttings of well-ripened young shoots may be struck in a frame or in a sheltered spot outdoors in autumn.

There are so many fine barberries that it is difficult to make a reasonably small selection. Among the evergreens *B. Darwinii* should certainly be grown. It makes a big bush with small, shining green, prickly leaves like holly leaves on a tiny scale, and it bears hanging clusters of orange flowers in April and early May. I regard it as among the best dozen evergreens for the garden.

Equally good is *B. stenophylla*, rather looser and more arching in habit than *B. Darwinii*, with much narrower leaves and yellow flowers, produced a week or so later. Unlike *B. Darwinii* it is easy to transplant. *B. buxifolia*, in the same group is less effective.

Then there is *B. lologensis*, with apricot yellow flowers and *B. linearifolia*, like an even more free flowering and brilliantly red-orange *B. Darwinii*, but slow in growth and not always satisfactory. It is a grand shrub where it succeeds.

To this brief list I would add *B. Gagnepainii* for its very handsome clusters of lance-shaped leaves and *B. verruculosa* for its extremely dense habit and leaves like those of *B. Darwinii*.

Of the deciduous kinds *B. Jamesiana* is notable for its very long, grape-like clusters of berries, pale green in summer, changing to coral in autumn. It is a tall shrub with long, arching branches. I would also select *B. Wilsonae* for its dense yet graceful growth and magnificent crops of coral red berries. Often it does not exceed 3 feet in height.

B. aggregata Prattii and *B. polyantha* have extra large clusters of fruit, while *B. rubrostilla* has very large, long berries and *B. Thunbergii* has brilliantly coloured leaves in autumn. *B. vulgaris*, the British barberry, has a dangerous addiction to rust disease.

BERGENIA *(Large-leaved Saxifrage)*

These plants were at one time united with the saxifrage by botanists. Nevertheless they are very different in appearance, with their large, thick usually round or oval leaves, and their short, rather clumsily formed spikes of pink flowers produced early in the year. Their very early flowering season and the handsome, almost evergreen, character of their foliage makes the bergenias good garden plants. They will thrive in full sun or partial shade and in any soil, in fact they make very good town garden plants. All are readily increased by division after flowering.

The best kinds are *B. cordifolia* and *B. crassifolia*, both about 18 inches in height, and *B. ligulata* and *B. Stracheyi*, nearer one foot.

BOUGAINVILLEA

Unfortunately *Bougainvillea glabra*, a brilliant climber from Brazil, is too tender to be grown outdoors in this country. In

Mediterranean countries it has established itself so firmly that it is one of the commonest climbers. There are also numerous garden varieties of this and of *B. spectabilis*, some, like Mrs. Butt, with pink flowers, and some, like Louie Wathin, orange. All are lovely but none exceeds the species in brilliance.

Bougainvilleas should be grown in greenhouses or conservatories with a minimum winter temperature of 45°. They may be grown in pots but are happier in a border of good soil, where their abundant stems can be trained, without too much restriction or pruning, to the rafters. If they must be kept to a limited space, prune them each February by cutting back all the previous year's growth to within an inch or so of the main vines, in the same way as grape vines under glass.

They appreciate plenty of water in summer. The temperature then should average 65° and it does not matter if it runs up much higher sometimes. Propagation is by cuttings of firm young shoots pulled off in spring with a heel of older wood, and rooted in sandy soil in a close frame with bottom heat in temperature of around 70° until roots are formed.

BRACHYCOME *(Swan River Daisy)*

Brachycome iberidifolia, a pretty South African annual, produces blue, pink or white daisy-like flowers freely in summer on a dwarf bushy plant, usually little over a foot high. It is raised from seed sown in a greenhouse or frame in March or early April, the seedlings being pricked off and later hardened in a frame for planting outdoors in June. It is also possible to sow in early May direct in the beds in which the plants are to flower. It likes warm sunny places and open, well-drained soils.

BUDDLEIA *(Butterfly Bush)*

The purple buddleia is one of the commonest and best of summer flowering shrubs. It has naturalized itself in many places, filling waste areas with its loosely-formed bushes covered in July and August by the long, tapering spikes of mauve or purple flowers. This is *Buddleia Davidii*, a grand shrub which used to be known as *B. variabilis*. Numerous garden varieties have been raised of which two of the best are Ile de France and Royal Red, both with very deep purple flowers. There are also white flowered forms but these are not so decorative. Another useful variety is *nanhoensis*, only about half the height of the common buddleia, with elegant flower spikes.

All delight in sun and good drainage and thrive in the poorest of soils, even finding roothold in walls. They need not be pruned, but for the finest spikes of bloom the previous year's stems should be cut back each March to within a few inches of the older wood.

Two very different species are *B. alternifolia* and *B. globosa*. The former makes a big bush, with long slender arching stems wreathed with small purple flowers in June. It is more graceful but not as spectacular as *B. Davidii*.

B. globosa has much the same open habit as *B. Davidii*

Bougainvillea spectabilis

Brachycome iberidifolia

Buddleia madagascariensis

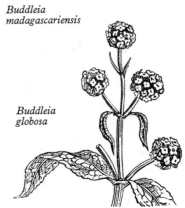

Buddleia globosa

Calceolaria Fothergillii

Calceolaria amplexicaulis

Calceolaria biflora

Calceolaria crenatiflora

(both are apt to get somewhat gaunt if left unpruned) but instead of purple spikes it has orange coloured balls, rather less than an inch in diameter, in June. It is not as good a shrub as either of the other species, but is unusual and worth growing.

All these can be increased by cuttings of well-ripened young stems inserted in a frame or a sheltered place outdoors in the autumn.

CALCEOLARIA *(Slipper Flower)*

Calceolarias need to be considered in two quite distinct groups, the half-shrubby and nearly hardy kinds used for summer bedding, and the soft-stemmed (herbaceous) kinds grown in greenhouses. All have the curious, pouch-like flowers characteristic of the genus, which are quite small in the bedding calceolarias, but often very large and showy in the greenhouse varieties.

Because of their very different growth the two groups need quite different treatment. The bedding calceolarias are raised from cuttings, usually taken in early autumn and rooted in an unheated frame, whereas the greenhouse varieties are treated as annuals and raised from seed every year. The seed is sown in June or July in pots, pans or boxes in an unheated greenhouse. The seedlings are pricked off as soon as they can be handled and a few weeks later potted singly in small pots. All this time they are happier in a frame than a greenhouse as they like a cool moist atmosphere. But in October, as soon as sharp frost threatens, they must be removed to a greenhouse and grown on steadily in a temperature of 45° to 55° to flower the following spring. They will need 5 to 8-inch pots in which to flower, according to the size of the plants, and they may have their last potting in early March. For all these pottings John Innes compost may be used. Avoid hot, dry atmospheres, shade the plants from strong sunshine, and water fairly freely, without allowing water to collect at the bases of the leaves.

There are many varieties or strains all with handsomely blotched flowers in shades of yellow and red.

Bedding calceolarias only need frost protection in a frame from October to early May when they can be planted out where they are to flower. There are two principal varieties, one with yellow and the other with chestnut red flowers.

CALENDULA *(Pot Marigold)*

This is one of the easiest flowers to grow, a showy hardy annual which, once in the garden, will keep itself going for years by self-sown seed. But the many fine modern varieties tend to deteriorate rapidly when grown in this way. After a few years the flowers will probably be nearly single and little different from those of the wild pot marigold. Good seed should be purchased each year and sown in March, April, May or September where the plants are to bloom the following summer. Thin to about a foot apart and thereafter leave them to themselves except for removing weeds and faded flowers.

26

Varieties differ in colour from yellow to deep orange. All have double flowers of varying form, some having flat petals and some quilled.

CALTHA *(Marsh Marigold, Kingcup)*

Caltha palustris, one of the loveliest of British bog plants, may be seen in many damp meadows or at streamsides in spring. The flowers are like very large buttercups carried on stout stems 1 to 2 feet in height. The leaves are broad and shining. It is well worth a place in the garden in very damp soil. The double-flowered form is interesting and showy but not as beautiful as the single-flowered wild form. There are also other species of which the best is *C. polypetala*, similar to the marsh marigold but with even larger flowers. Both can be increased by dividing their roots immediately after flowering, and this is also the best time at which to plant them.

Caltha palustris

CAMELLIA

This is a big family of evergreen shrubs and from *Camellia japonica* a great number of garden varieties has been produced, some with single flowers, some semi-double or anemone centred, and some fully double. They vary in colour from white and palest pink to scarlet and crimson and many are handsomely blotched with white on pink or red. All will make large shrubs, perhaps 15 feet or more in height and nearly as much through, but are usually seen as much smaller specimens and were once extensively cultivated as pot plants for the cool greenhouse or conservatory. Indeed it is only of recent years that the full hardiness of *C. japonica* has been realized and that it has begun to be planted outdoors at all extensively. Growth seldom gets cut by frost, even in very cold places, but the flowers are sensitive to frost and as they are produced very early in the spring (sometimes even in winter) the plants should be given a fairly sheltered position if possible. They will thrive in full sun or in partial shade and they like slightly acid soils such as those that suit rhododendrons and azaleas. They need no pruning and, once established, may be left entirely alone except for an occasional mulch of grass mowings or compost to keep them well fed.

In addition to *C. japonica* and its varieties, there are some other good kinds but these are not all so hardy. *C. saluenensis*, one of the most reliable, is a lovely shrub with evergreen leaves smaller than those of *C. japonica* and more fragile single pink flowers, rather like single roses. It has produced a grand race of hybrids with *C. japonica*, the lilac pink J. C. Williams being one of the best. One advantage of all these kinds is that these single flowers fall when they fade instead of remaining on the bush as a disfigurement as so often happens with the double-flowered forms of *C. japonica*.

Another magnificent species is *C. reticulata* which has very large, usually semi-double, rose-pink flowers. It makes a very big shrub, looser and more sprawling in habit than *C. japonica*,

Camellia reticulata

Camellia Sasanqua plena

Camellia japonica

27

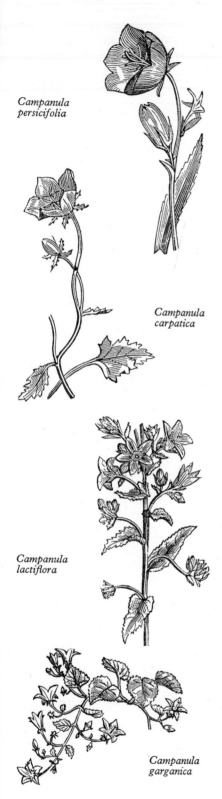

*Campanula
persicifolia*

*Campanula
carpatica*

*Campanula
lactiflora*

*Campanula
garganica*

but it is tender and really a shrub for the mild counties such as Devon and Cornwall.

Varieties of *C. japonica* can be increased by cuttings of firm young growth taken in July and rooted in a close frame. Varieties of *C. reticulata* and some other camellias must be grafted in spring on to seedlings of *C. japonica*.

CAMPANULA *(Bellflower)*

Another big family, which spreads itself into rock garden and herbaceous border as well as providing in the familiar Canterbury bell an excellent plant for bedding.

It is difficult to generalize about campanulas because they are so numerous and so different, but most of them are easy plants to grow in ordinary soil and open position. Many will even tolerate a measure of shade. Almost all can be readily increased by dividing their roots in spring or autumn and most can also be raised from seed sown in spring in frame or greenhouse. A slightly different method is required for the Canterbury bell (*Campanula Medium*) a biennial, seed of which should be sown in a frame or in a sheltered place outdoors in May or early June. The seedlings are pricked out, about 6 inches apart, in a nursery bed where they can grow on into fine clumps for removal in September or October to their flowering quarters.

One of the best of the herbaceous bellflowers is *C. persicifolia*. It spreads fairly fast making low clumps of narrow leaves above which stand, each June and July, the 2 to 3–foot high slender stems bearing numerous large nodding bell shaped usually lavender blue flowers. There are deeper coloured and white forms and some with double flowers.

Another good plant, which does well in shady places, is *C. lactiflora*. This is 5 feet in height and produces, in July and August, large, loose sprays of small, widely opened bells, either pale blue or near-white.

C. latiloba, also known as *C. grandis*, is a much stiffer and less elegant plant with 2 to 3–foot spikes of blue flowers in June and July. It will grow well in practically any place.

The two finest rock garden bellflowers are *C. Portenschlagiana* (*C. muralis*), and *C. cochleariflora* (*C. pusilla*). The first makes great sheets of small shining green leaves down any retaining wall on which it is planted, completely covering these in May and June with its widely opened purple flowers. I regard it as one of the twelve best rock plants. *C. cochlearifolia*, a more fragile plant with thread-like stems 3 or 4 inches high, bears nodding bells of blue or white.

CANNA *(Indian Shot)*

These are tropical plants with large, handsome, upstanding leaves usually either rich green or purplish in colour, and bold spikes of gaudily coloured flowers, usually red or yellow variously splashed and spotted with one colour on the other. They are not difficult to grow as they have fleshy roots which can be stored in a frost-proof greenhouse during the winter and re-started

*Canna
iridiflora*

*Caryopteris
Mastacanthus*

*Catananche
caerulea*

*Ceanothus
thyrsiflorus*

into growth in spring in a temperature around 60°. It is best to pot the roots individually in pots large enough to accommodate them comfortably. They can, if preferred, be grown in pots throughout and used for greenhouse or conservatory decoration or, alternatively, they can be bedded out in June as soon as all danger of frost is past. They should have a sunny position, a fairly rich soil and abundant water. Directly frost threatens, outdoor plants should be lifted, boxed or potted and returned to the greenhouse where they can be gradually dried off ready for storing again. It is best to keep them in soil all the time even when they are completely without water. Propagation is by division of the roots in spring or by seeds sown in spring, but seeds are hard and need thorough soaking and a fairly high temperature to germinate them.

CARYOPTERIS *(Blue Spiraea)*

The popular name is not inappropriate in that it gives some idea of the appearance of this attractive shrub with its rather fluffy looking clusters of blue flowers in early autumn.

The best kind for the garden is *C. clandonensis*, a hybrid with blue flowers, and a fine vigorous habit which makes it more generally reliable than the better known of its parents, *C. Mastacanthus*. Unpruned it will make a loose bush, 3 or 4 feet high, but it can be cut back quite severely each April when it will branch freely and make a much more compact plant perhaps 2½ feet in height. It is easily increased by cuttings of firm young growth, taken at practically any time in summer and rooted in a frame.

CATANANCHE *(Cupid's Dart)*

The only species grown in gardens is *Catananche caerulea*, a hardy herbaceous plant that might be mistaken at first for some kind of cornflower. It has similar lavender-blue flowers but they are silvery underneath and the petals feel dry and chaffy. It grows about 2 feet high and flowers in late summer. It is quite hardy but does not like winter wet and is most permanent in rather poor, well-drained soils. The flowers are useful for cutting and, with care, will last some time though they are not true 'everlastings'. Propagation is by division of the roots in spring or autumn.

CEANOTHUS *(Californian Lilac)*

These are very beautiful shrubs mostly with blue flowers, though there are pink and white kinds. The individual flowers, usually quite small, are carried in clusters neat and thimble-like in the evergreen kinds such as *Ceanothus Burkwoodii*, *C. dentatus*, *C. rigidus*, *C. thyrsiflorus* and *C. Veitchianus*, or larger, looser and more cone-shaped in the deciduous *C. azureus* and its numerous garden forms or hybrids. The evergreen kinds mostly flower in spring, though *C. Burkwoodii* blooms continuously all the summer. *C. azureus* and the varieties associated with it, are all late summer flowering. While most of the evergreen kinds are happiest against a sunny wall, the deciduous kinds are seen to

29

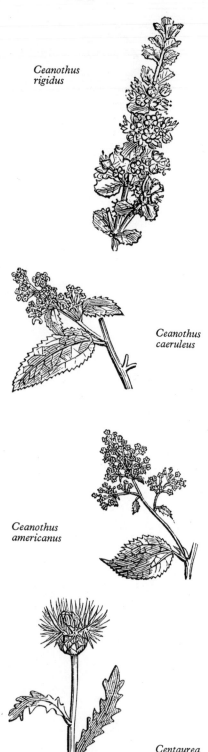

*Ceanothus
rigidus*

*Ceanothus
caeruleus*

*Ceanothus
americanus*

*Centaurea
moschata*

better advantage in a bed or border in which they have room to expand. Once again *C. Burkwoodii* occupies a midway position, for though it can be grown against a wall, it is equally happy in the shrub border.

Sharp frost may injure many species but usually the hybrids of *C. azureus* and *C. americanus* are unharmed and this is also true of *C. thyrsiflorus*. Among the best of the *C. azureus* varieties and hybrids are Gloire de Versailles, light blue; Indigo and Topaz, both deep blue; and Perle Rose, pink.

All like well-drained soils. The evergreen kinds may be cut back a little after flowering to keep them in shape, and the deciduous kinds can be pruned back quite severely each March if desired. They will then make strong, cane-like growths carrying flower trusses of extra size. *C. Burkwoodii* is best pruned in April.

Propagation is by cuttings of firm young growth taken in July or August and rooted in a close frame.

CELOSIA *(Cockscomb, Prince of Wales's Feather)*

The most popular varieties are derived from *C. argentea* and carry feathery plumes of yellow, scarlet or crimson flowers on stems 12 to 18 inches in height. In the curious cockscomb (*C. argentea cristata*) the crimson flowers are huddled together to form a compact, twisted mass not unlike the comb of a cock.

All are half-hardy annuals flowering throughout the latter half of the summer. They need a fair amount of warmth in the early stages and seed should be sown in January or February in a temperature of 65° to 70°, the seedlings being grown on singly in small pots in rich soil, and potted on to 4-inch pots as they need more room. They must be carefully hardened off for planting outdoors in June. They should be given as sunny and sheltered a position as possible. Alternatively celosias may be grown as pot plants for summer flowering in the greenhouse.

CENTAUREA *(Cornflower, Sweet Sultan)*

The centaureas may be considered in three distinct groups; the hardy annual varieties, the hardy herbaceous perennials and the slightly tender grey-leaved perennials, popular in summer bedding schemes.

Best known of the annuals is the common cornflower, *Centaurea Cyanus*. It grows 3 or 4 feet in height and has bright blue flowers, but there are also pink, lilac, pale blue and white varieties as well as dwarf varieties not exceeding 1 foot in height. All can be raised from seed, sown in March, April, May or September, where the plants are to flower. They like open sunny places but are not fussy about soil. They will need thinning to about 9 inches apart and supporting with some hazel branches or similar brushy material. The dwarf varieties need only be thinned to 6 inches and will not require support. The tall varieties are admirable for cutting.

Another useful annual is the sweet sultan, *Centaurea moschata*, averaging 18 inches in height, with fragrant flowers individually larger than those of the cornflower and in a wider range of colours, including yellow, mauve, various shades of purple, wine red and white. It is a little more difficult to grow as although it may be sown outdoors in March, April or September, where the plants are to flower the following summer, a little more care must be taken to prepare a good, crumbly, easily worked seed bed. Thin the seedlings to about 9 inches. They will not need any support. The sweet sultan likes sun and warmth and is not so robustly hardy as the cornflower.

The hardy perennial centaureas are not on the whole so well known, though *C. montana*, with its starry blue cornflowers produced on 18-inch stems in May, is seen fairly frequently. It also has a white form.

Another good perennial species is *C. dealbata*, about 2 feet in height, with rosy-pink flowers in June and July. *C. macrocephala*, 4 feet in height, has yellow flowers 4 inches in diameter, and *C. ruthenica*, a smaller yellow flowered kind, has handsome, deeply cut leaves.

All these hardy perennials will grow in any ordinary soil and fairly open position and can be increased by division in either spring or autumn.

In the grey-leaved bedding centaureas, *C. Cineraria*, *C. gymnocarpa*, and *C. ragusina*, the flowers are unimportant as they are grown for the beauty of their deeply cut, grey or nearly white leaves. They are often used as a foil for the bright colours of 'geraniums', scarlet salvias and similar flowers. They can be increased by cuttings in spring or early autumn, and should be given frame or greenhouse protection in winter.

CENTRANTHUS (Red Valerian)

The common red valerian, *Centranthus ruber*, one of the best plants for dry walls, cliff faces and other stony places provided there is plenty of room for it, may be seen growing wild in many parts of the country. It is a hardy perennial, about two feet in height, producing its small rosy-pink flowers in fine heads throughout June and July with some odd spikes appearing later in the summer. It is so trouble-free and decorative that it is well worth planting wherever there is a suitable spot for it. Good drainage is essential and it really does not matter how poor and stony the soil may be.

There is a white flowered variety and another with much brighter, nearly crimson, flowers, which is usually named '*coccineus*'. All can be increased by careful division in spring or autumn, or by cuttings of firm young shoots rooted in a frame in early spring or summer.

CERATOSTIGMA

These are very closely related to the leadworts (plumbago), indeed at one time they were known as plumbago. Of the two kinds commonly grown *Ceratostigma plumbaginoides* (*Larpentae*) is a herbaceous perennial and *C. Willmottianum* is a shrub which is often killed to ground level in winter but shoots up again from

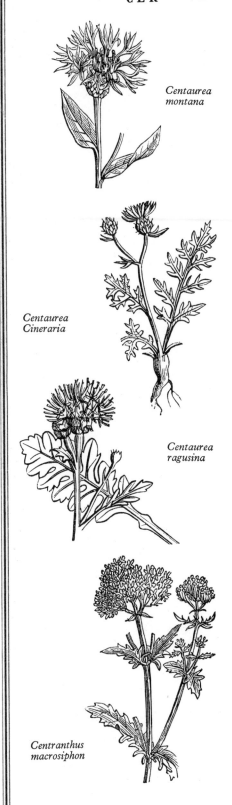

Centaurea montana

Centaurea Cineraria

Centaurea ragusina

Centranthus macrosiphon

31

*Ceratostigma
plumbaginoides*

*Chaenomeles
japonica*

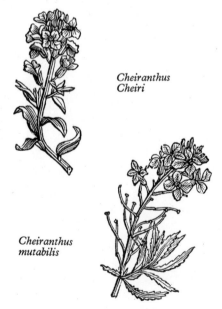

*Cheiranthus
Cheiri*

*Cheiranthus
mutabilis*

basal buds like a herbaceous plant. Both are valued for their blue flowers, shaped like those of a phlox and extremely pure and bright in colour. *C. plumbaginoides*, about 1 foot in height and spreading in habit, flowers in late summer. *C. Willmottianum* may reach 3 or 4 feet in a sheltered place where it does not get cut by frost. More often it is seen as a spreading bush about 1½ to 2 feet in height. It will flower from July to November in a favourable season and is worthy of a good situation, in a sheltered, sunny border with good but well-drained soil. Both can usually be increased by careful division in the spring and *C. Willmottianum* also by cuttings taken in July and rooted in a frame.

CHAENOMELES *(Japanese Quince)*

Many gardeners simply know this as 'japonica'. It has suffered from having too many different names, and even to-day is frequently listed as *Cydonia japonica* though its correct name is *Chaenomeles lagenaria*. It flowers in early spring and the commonest variety has brilliant scarlet flowers, though there are also white, pink, and crimson forms. Though perfectly hardy and capable of making a densely branched bush in the shrub border, it is most frequently seen trained against walls where it certainly looks well as the flowers benefit from the protection. Grown in this way it will want a little careful pruning after flowering, to get rid of surplus growth, and training to spread it out fanwise on the wall. It will grow to 10 feet under favourable conditions.

A similar species, often called *Cydonia Maulei* but which should really be *Chaenomeles japonica*, is dwarfer in habit, rarely exceeding 3 feet in height, with orange-scarlet flowers. A very fine form named *Simonii* has rich crimson flowers.

The Japanese Quinces are shrubs for sunny places but are not at all fussy about soil. All can be increased by layering in spring or early summer. All flower in May.

CHEIRANTHUS *(Wallflower)*

Our old friend the wallflower looks a little strange under its botanical title, *Cheiranthus Cheiri*. Everyone loves it for its showy and richly scented flowers in spring, and it is a universal favourite for spring bedding. For this it is grown as a biennial, though in fact it is a herbaceous perennial and old clumps of it are to be seen on many walls or in rocky places. But in the richer and less well drained soil of the garden it is apt to get soft and be badly damaged by frost in winter and for bedding it is more convenient to throw the plants away when they have finished flowering and raise a fresh batch for next year. This is done by sowing seed outdoors in May, pricking the seedlings out at least 6 inches apart into a nursery bed, finally transferring them in October to their flowering quarters.

There are many varieties varying in the colour of their flowers, through shades of yellow, chestnut red, crimson and a rather curious purplish-mauve. In addition there are other species such as *C. mutabilis*, purple and cream.

Bergenia cordifolia

Artemisia luctiflora

Azalea [Ghent hybrid]

Bougainvillea Louie Wathin

Aubrieta [garden form]

Aster Frikartii

Begonia Rex [leaf]

Arum [Zantedeschia aethiopica]

Bellis perennis [garden form]

Astilbe Arendsii

Berberis Darwinii

Berberis polyantha

Begonia [double flowered garden form]

CNT

Camellia japonica

Campanula
cochleariifolia

Calceolaria
integrifolia

Caryopteri
clandonens

Buddleia Davidii

Canna indica

Caryanche
caerulea

Brachycome
iberidifolia

Ceanoth
Burkwoo

Campanula
Medium

Calendula
officinalis

Caltha
palustris

Celosia
plumosa

CNF

CHIMONANTHUS *(Winter Sweet)*

This is a deciduous shrub often heard of but seldom seen, no doubt because, though its fragrant flowers are produced in mid-winter, they are not at all showy and may even pass unnoticed until one is attracted to them by their scent. Moreover though *Chimonanthus fragrans* is itself reasonably hardy, its flowers are readily damaged by frost and it is best against a wall except in the mildest parts of the country. Unpruned it makes a big, open bush but with a little judicious pruning each year after flowering, it can easily be trained as a wall shrub. The flowers are pale yellow and semi-transparent and they have purplish-maroon centres. A variety, *luteus*, has primrose yellow flowers lacking the purple centre. Both will grow in ordinary soil and can be increased by seed sown in spring or by layers in late summer.

CHIONODOXA *(Glory of the Snow)*

Very attractive small bulbous-rooted spring flowering plants. Two of the best are *Chionodoxa Luciliae* and *C. sardensis*, both with starry flowers in loose clusters on 8-inch stems but whereas the flowers of *C. Luciliae* are bright blue with a white centre, those of *C. sardensis* are a deeper blue throughout. The bulbs should be planted 3 inches deep in September or October, in ordinary soil either in full sun or partial shade and thereafter left undisturbed for years. They will gradually increase in number and become progressively more lovely. If bulbs are required elsewhere one or two clumps may be lifted in July or August, divided into single bulbs, and replanted. These are excellent plants for the rock garden.

CHOISYA *(Mexican Orange)*

Choisya ternata is a first-class evergreen shrub but it will not stand a great deal of frost. In milder parts and near the coast it is usually quite safe, but in colder places it may need the protection of a wall. With that one exception it has all the virtues; attractive, glossy foliage, an excellent rounded habit, fine clusters of white flowers very like orange blossom, fragrance, and a long flowering season. It is at its best in May but may carry some flowers from April to September. It is not fussy about soil and, though it likes sun, will grow in partial shade. It can be easily increased by cuttings of firm young growth inserted in a frame between July and September inclusive.

CHRYSANTHEMUM

This is one of the great families of the flower garden, so rich in its diversity that many books have been devoted to it alone.

Broadly speaking chrysanthemums may be considered under four main headings, annual varieties flowering in summer and readily raised from seed sown in spring where the plants are to bloom, hardy border perennials, Japanese chrysanthemums derived from *C. morifolium* which may themselves be divided into two sections, one for outdoor and the other for greenhouse

C

33

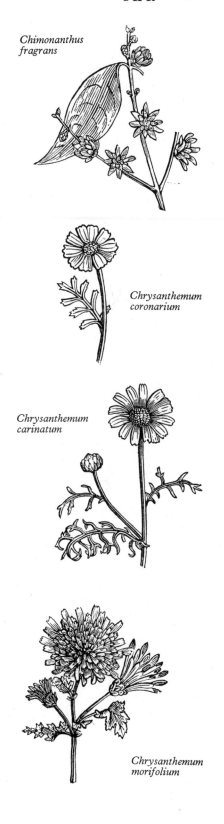

Chimonanthus fragrans

Chrysanthemum coronarium

Chrysanthemum carinatum

Chrysanthemum morifolium

Chrysanthemum
(reflexed)

Chrysanthemum
(incurving)

Chrysanthemum
(anemone-centred)

Chrysanthemum
(pompon)

cultivation, and the half-hardy, semi-shrubby varieties of which the common marguerite (*Chrysanthemum frutescens*) is the best-known example.

The annuals, *C. carinatum* and *C. coronarium*, will grow freely in any soil and reasonably open situation. All have daisy-like flowers on good stems, heights varying from 1½ to 3 feet. Some are single, some double-flowered and the ground colour is usually white or yellow though often this is banded with crimson or maroon. Among the best hardy annuals for summer flowering in the garden, they make excellent cut flowers. For an extra early display seed should be sown in September where the plants are to flower the following year. Seedlings should be thinned to 1 foot apart.

The hardy herbaceous chrysanthemums are familiarly known as moon daisies (or ox-eye daisies) and shasta daisies, the former being varieties of our own native *Chrysanthemum Leucanthemum*, a beautiful weed in meadows, and the latter varieties of the Pyrenean *C. maximum*. Here again there are double as well as single-flowered forms but all are white or at most no more than cream and all flower in June and July. Heights vary between 2 and 3 feet. Propagation is by division in spring.

The Japanese chrysanthemums are the most varied of all and thousands of varieties have been raised. Every year sees scores of new ones added to the list. In addition to the two great divisions already noted, into outdoor and indoor kinds, chrysanthemums are also classified according to the shape and size of their flowers. There are single-flowered varieties, doubles which may be reflexed (that is the petals curling outwards and downwards) or incurving (that is the petals curling inwards). The most perfect of the latter, which form almost completely globular flowers, are known as incurved. Intermediate between the singles and doubles are anemone-centred varieties which have an outer ring of single petals and a pincushion-like centre of fluted or tubular petals.

A further division is made according to size, decoratives being of intermediate size suitable for garden display or arranging in the house and exhibition varieties being larger. Smallest of all are the pompons, often with flowers little over an inch in diameter.

For details of cultivation the reader is referred to specialist books on the subject.

Finally there is the marguerite of which there is a primrose yellow variety as well as the familiar white. These are the popular 'daisies' used for summer bedding. They make fine bushy plants and will flower continuously all through the summer. They can be increased by cuttings rooted in a frame or greenhouse at almost any time of the year except winter.

CINERARIA

There are no more showy plants for the cool greenhouse than the cinerarias (*Senecio cruentus*). All have single daisy flowers carried in big, loose clusters, the colour range embracing all shades of blue and purple, pink and crimson, some with broad white bands of white which make the colour seem even more brilliant. There are two principal groups, one the large-flowered cinerarias in which the individual blooms are 3 or 4 inches in diameter, and the other the star-flowered or stellata varieties in which the individual flowers are much smaller though there are more of them in every cluster. Both are useful, the stellata varieties perhaps being better for decorative arrangements because of their lightness, the large-flowered varieties being superior where a mass of colour is required.

All are treated as annuals, seed being sown under glass some time between April and early July according to the time the plants are to flower. From the earliest sowings November flowers will be obtained and from the latest plants that will bloom in April or May. Very little heat is required, and throughout the plants should be grown as though they were nearly hardy. The seedlings must be pricked off and later potted singly, first in small pots, later in 4- or 5-inch pots and finally into the 6-, 7- or 8- inch pots in which they will flower. From June to early October the plants will be happier in a frame and will need little protection. When they are returned to the greenhouse in the autumn they should be ventilated freely whenever the weather is favourable, and be watered carefully. Leaf mining maggots sometimes disfigure the leaves badly but can be kept in check by occasional spraying with nicotine.

CISTUS *(Rock Rose)*

Rock rose, although officially the popular name of the cistuses, is used frequently for the helianthemums, which causes a good deal of confusion. The two genera are very closely allied, the most obvious difference from the garden standpoint being that whereas almost all the helianthemums are sprawling plants most suitable for rock garden or dry wall, the cistuses are far more definitely shrubs, with strong woody stems which often form big bushes 5 or 6 feet in height and even more in diameter. All have rather fragile saucer-shaped flowers and though the individual blooms do not last long, they are so freely replaced by opening buds that the display continues for several weeks in June and July with some stragglers appearing right on into the autumn.

The cistuses are evergreen and would be in the very front rank of shrubs if they were a little hardier. Few kinds are completely reliable in the colder parts of the country. They will survive mild winters but will be killed in a really hard winter. Nevertheless they are so readily and rapidly renewable, either from seed sown in spring or by cuttings taken in summer, that they are worth a slight risk. All like well-drained soils and seem not to mind how poor it may be. They are ideal for hot stony or gravelly places in full sun. No pruning is required.

The hardiest kind is probably *Cistus laurifolius* with pure white flowers but even more showy is *C. cyprius* a fine hybrid with large white, purple-blotched flowers. *C. ladaniferus*, often known as the gum cistus because of its sticky leaves, is one of the parents

35

Cistus ladaniferus

Cistus purpureus

Cistus cyprius

Cistus laurifolius

Clarkia
elegans

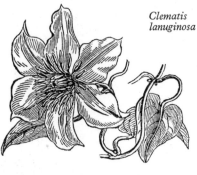

Clematis
lanuginosa

Clematis
indivisa

Clematis
heracleifolia

of *C. cyprius* and equally beautiful but not so hardy. Its flowers are white either with or without a purple blotch.

Handsome but rather tender is *C. purpureus* with very large rosy-purple flowers with a maroon blotch. Where it succeeds it will make a big bush in time. Smaller and more delicate in colouring, and also, I think, rather more hardy, is the lovely hybrid *C. Silver Pink. C. crispus* and *C. albidus* have deeper magenta flowers.

CLARKIA

One of the best and hardiest of annuals, clarkias can be sown outdoors in March, April, May or September where they will flower from May to September according to the time at which they were sown. They will need a little thinning out and weeding. They do not seem to mind what soil they are grown in and they will even flower tolerably well in shady places.

Clarkias produce long, slender spikes of double flowers, pink, brick red or white, individually rather shapeless, but attractive in the mass. Heights vary from $1\frac{1}{2}$ to 3 feet and seedlings should be thinned accordingly, the shorter varieties to 9 inches the taller to 1 foot or thereabouts.

CLEMATIS (Virgin's Bower)

The purple *Clematis Jackmanii*, with its tangled but slender growths and great masses of large rich purple flowers in July and August, is justly one of the most popular of hardy climbers.

There are many other kinds differing in the size of their flowers, their colour and their time of flowering. One of the earliest is the evergreen *C. Armandii*, with masses of small white flowers in March or April.

A little later, in May, comes *C. montana*, another small-flowered kind, typically white though there are also pink forms.

Later still, flowering from June to October, come a great many beautiful hybrids, mostly with rather large single or double flowers, from white and palest lavender or pink, to intense purple and carmine. A few good varieties are Comtesse de Bouchaud, double pale pink; Ernest Markham, petunia red; Henryi, white; Lady Northcliffe, lavender and blue; Lasurstern, purplish-blue; Nelly Moser, mauve and red; Perle d'Azur, double light blue; Ville de Lyon, carmine, and Duchess of Edinburgh double white. These come from such species as *CC. florida, Jackmanii, lanuginosa, patens* and *viticella.*

An uncommon but beautiful clematis is *C. tangutica* with small lantern-shaped yellow flowers followed by silvery seed heads.

All these thrive in rich soils that hold moisture without becoming waterlogged. That may explain their fondness for chalk soils for these usually possess such characteristics. Another peculiarity is that although they like to have their roots in the shade they prefer to have their heads in the sun. This can often be arranged either by screening them with a shrub which will shade their roots, or by planting them in the shady side of a building but training their shoots round to the sunny side.

The very vigorous kinds do not need regular pruning but some

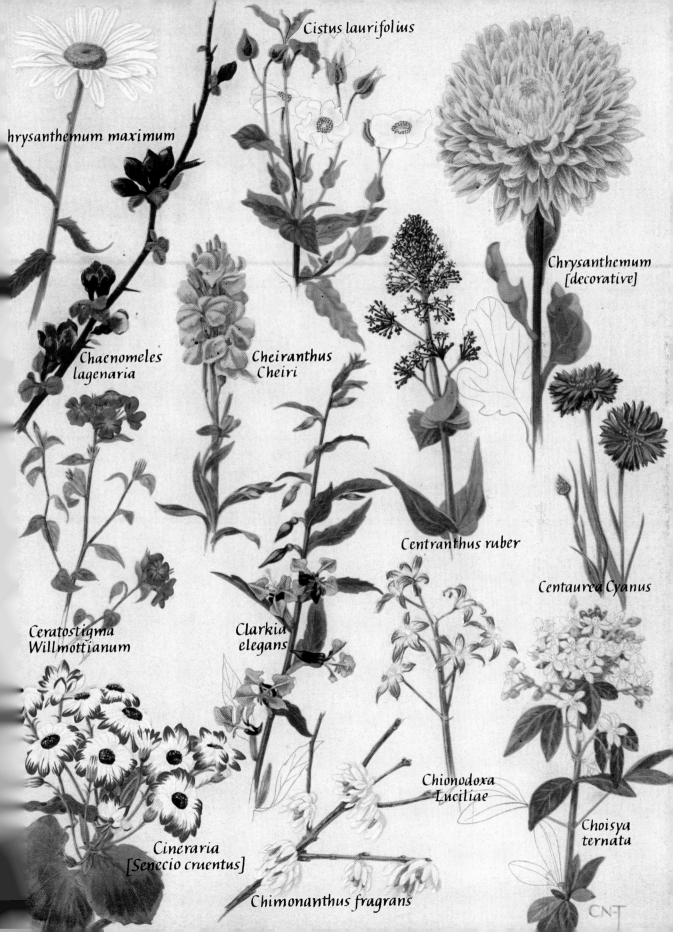

Cistus laurifolius

hrysanthemum maximum

Chrysanthemum
[decorative]

Chaenomeles
lagenaria

Cheiranthus
Cheiri

Centranthus ruber

Centaurea Cyanus

Ceratostigma
Willmottianum

Clarkia
elegans

Chionodoxa
Luciliae

Choisya
ternata

Cineraria
[Senecio cruentus]

Chimonanthus fragrans

CNT

Clianthus
Dampieri

Convolvulus
minor

Clematis
[garden form]

Cobaea
scandens

Clerodendrum
trichotomum

Clivia
miniata

Clerodendrum
Fargesii

Collinsia
bicolor

Cleome
spinosa

Coreopsis
lanceolata

Convallaria
majalis

Colchicum
autumnale

Cornus Kousa

Coleus Blumei
[garden form]

of the weaker varieties should be pruned annually in February. The previous year's growth may then be shortened quite severely, even as much as to within a few inches of the main vines. Care should be taken to make each cut just above a bud that is just starting into growth.

All these clematis can be increased by layering in early summer and the species, such as *C. Armandii*, *C. montana* and *C. tangutica*, can also be increased readily from seed sown in a greenhouse or frame in spring.

There are also herbaceous species such as *C. heracleifolia* and *C. recta* which are increased by careful division.

Clematis patens

CLEOME *(Spider Flower)*

An uncommon but beautiful half-hardy annual which makes a big plant about 4 feet in height carrying loose spikes of pink flowers with very narrow petals and long stamens which give them a curiously spidery appearance. A fine plant for the centre of a large bed or for a back position in borders devoted to annuals or summer bedding plants, it may also be used effectively to fill gaps in the herbaceous border. It flowers in July or August.

Seed should be sown in a greenhouse or frame in February or March and the seedlings pricked off and then hardened off in a frame in readiness for planting out in May. *C. spinosa*, the kind usually grown, likes sun but is not particular about soil.

Clematis florida

CLERODENDRUM *(Glory Tree)*

Clerodendrums may be conveniently divided into two groups, the tender kinds only suitable for warm greenhouses, and the hardy or nearly hardy shrubs which can be grown outdoors. In the former group are *C. Thomsoniae* (syn. *C. Balfouri*) and *C. fallax*; in the latter group are *C. Bungei* (syn. *C. foetidum*) and *C. trichotomum*.

C. Thomsoniae, an evergreen climber bearing loose sprays of fine crimson and white flowers in summer, can be grown in a tub or large pot but is really happier planted in a greenhouse border of moderately rich soil. Given plenty of room to be trained under the greenhouse rafters, it will soon make a fine specimen and require little pruning. Alternatively it can be trained over a crinoline-like frame and kept to this restricted size by being pruned immediately after flowering. All young shoots should be shortened to about 3 inches.

C. fallax, a shrubby plant, is most commonly raised from seed and discarded after flowering as if it were an annual. Seed sown in warmth in February will give plants that will produce their vivid orange-red flowers the following autumn. A second sowing can be made in August and the seedlings from this will flower from June to August the following year. But as these plants like a temperature that never falls below 50°, a good deal of artificial heat will be required.

C. Bungei and *C. trichotomum* are both shrubs. *C. Bungei* with clusters of rosy-red flowers in late summer is less hardy than *C. trichotomum* which has loose sprays of white and reddish-

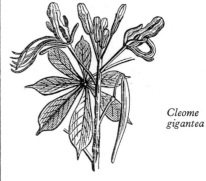

Cleome gigantea

Clerodendrum splendens

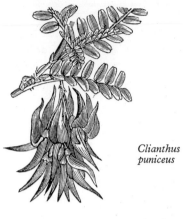

*Clianthus
puniceus*

*Clianthus
Dampieri*

*Clivia
nobilis*

*Cobaea
scandens*

brown flowers in late summer, followed in a favourable season by blue berries. These shrubs like warm sheltered places. They can be increased by cuttings of firm young growth in July.

CLIANTHUS *(Glory Pea, Parrot's Bill, Lobster Claw)*

This always excites comment when in flower because of the extraordinary shape of its flower. Two of its popular names, parrot's bill and lobster claw are based on fancied resemblances and I think of the two the second comes nearest the mark. The hanging flowers are long, pointed and curved, not unlike a claw, crimson in the most familiar species, *Clianthus puniceus*, and scarlet with a nearly black blotch in the more difficult and weakly *C. Dampieri*.

Semi-trailing shrubs, of doubtful hardiness in most parts of the country, they may survive if trained against sunny, sheltered walls. Alternatively they can be grown in slightly heated greenhouses or conservatories, in large pots or tubs or planted in a border of good soil. Their rather weak stems should be given some support. Both flower in summer. They can be increased by seeds sown in a warm greenhouse.

CLIVIA *(Kaffir Lily)*

Clivia miniata, a showy and easily grown plant for the greenhouse, should be better known. Though not a true bulb, its fleshy roots are bulb-like and it can be increased by the removal of offsets in February. Alternatively it can be raised from seed sown in a cool greenhouse in spring but seedlings take several years to attain flowering size.

Clivias produce clusters of lily-like flowers on stout 2-foot stems in spring. Typically they are scarlet outside and yellow within, but there are many variations, some of the loveliest varieties being in shades of yellow or orange throughout. All need winter rest and should be kept nearly dry in a frost-proof greenhouse from November to January. Then they can be re-potted, if necessary, and watered more freely. In a temperature of 55° to 60° they will soon come into flower. From June to September they are happy in a frame, but should be returned to the greenhouse when frost threatens.

COBAEA *(Cups and Saucers)*

C. scandens, a vigorous climber usually treated as an annual, has green and purple bell shaped flowers not unlike Canterbury bells, though not so showy. They are produced freely in summer (usually in August and September outdoors). Seed is sown in a warm greenhouse in February or March, the seedlings are potted singly and hardened off in time for planting out in early June in a sunny place. They should be allowed to climb up a trellis or fence or over an archway or arbour which they will soon cover with their thin, clinging growths. After flowering the plants are left to be destroyed by frost. But they are, in fact, perennials and if grown in a frost-proof greenhouse will live for many years and eventually cover a considerable area.

COLCHICUM *(Autumn Crocus, Meadow Saffron)*

The common name, autumn crocus, is misleading as colchicums have no connexion with the true crocuses of which there are also autumn-flowering varieties. But the confusion is understandable as there is a strong superficial resemblance between the two flowers.

The bulbs of colchicum are very large but they do not, on that account, need to be planted very deep. It is sufficient to cover them with about 2 inches of soil. They should be planted in July or as early in August as the bulbs can be obtained, and thereafter, should be left undisturbed until over-crowding commences to impair their flowering. Ideal for naturalizing in grass, they may also be planted in large rock gardens, in borders, or at the front of shrubberies. They are mainly in shades of mauve pink but there are also fine white varieties and some that approach purple. Propagation is by division of the bulb clusters at planting time.

COLEUS

The coleus is an excellent greenhouse foliage plant for the beginner because it is so easily grown and has such variety. The hybrids commonly grown make soft-stemmed, bushy plants, with nettle-like leaves in a great diversity of colours and markings. They ask only for a frost-proof greenhouse and may even be kept in living rooms for considerable periods without harm. The John Innes compost suits them to perfection. Cuttings taken in spring or summer rarely fail to root in a close frame, or alternatively, they can be easily grown from seed sown in spring.

Two rather different species are *Coleus thyrsoideus* and *C. Frederici* which are cultivated for their long, slender spikes of purplish-blue flowers produced in winter. Cultivation is, on the whole, the same as for the ornamental-leaved varieties but in winter a temperature of about 55° will be needed to encourage flowering.

COLLINSIA

The collinsia commonly seen in gardens is *C. bicolor* a pretty hardy annual with neat parti-coloured flowers in shades of purple and white. It grows 9 to 12 inches high, flowers in summer and is a useful plant for the front or middle of annual borders. Sow seed from March to May for a succession of flowers, thinning the seedlings to about 9 inches and thereafter leaving them to grow undisturbed. A further sowing can be made in early September for May or June flowering the following year.

CONVALLARIA *(Lily of the Valley)*

The lily of the valley (*Convallaria majalis*) is so familiar to everyone that it can need no introduction or description, and I need only say that there is a pale pink flowered variety not nearly so beautiful as the common white.

It is a lover of cool, partially shady places and fairly rich, moist

Colchicum variegatum

Colchicum autumnale

Collinsia bicolor

Convallaria majalis

*Convolvulus
Cneorum*

*Convolvulus
althaeoides*

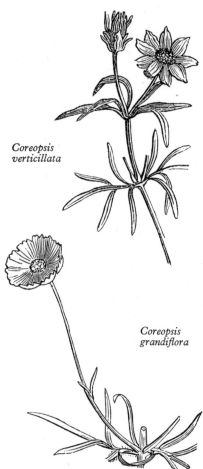

*Coreopsis
verticillata*

*Coreopsis
grandiflora*

(but not boggy) soils. It will often naturalize itself in thin woodland, provided it has not too much competition from weeds and grass. In the garden a bed on the shady side of a wall suits it well and it is a good thing to work in some well-rotted manure and leaf mould before planting.

The best time for planting is in October or March. The roots should be spread out thinly in drills and covered with about an inch of soil. Propagation is by division of the roots at planting time, but it is unwise to disturb the plants frequently. Leave them to spread and make a solid carpet of foliage and only lift when starvation through overcrowding brings about a falling off in flower production.

CONVOLVULUS *(Bindweed, Dwarf Morning Glory)*

One of the garden flowers listed as convolvulus, *C. major* (often called morning glory) will be found under Ipomoea on page 74.

C. minor (*tricolor*) is a beautiful hardy annual making a foot high, sprawling plant, bearing funnel-shaped blue, purple, pink or white flowers in summer. Seeds can be sown thinly in the open in March, April or September, where they are to bloom.

C. Cneorum is a 2 foot shrub with silvery leaves and white flowers in summer. It likes a warm sunny place and can be increased by summer cuttings inserted in a frame.

COREOPSIS *(Calliopsis, Tickseed)*

The different kinds of coreopsis may be considered in two groups, the hardy perennials and the hardy annuals.

The four best perennials are *C. lanceolata*, *C. auriculata*, *C. grandiflora* and *C. verticillata*. The first three have large, flat yellow flowers carried on slender 2-foot stems during most of the summer, but *C. grandiflora* has larger flowers than the others and also has some double or semi-double varieties (Perry's variety is a fine example of the last named), while *C. auriculata* differs in having a small crimson blotch at the base of each petal. All are inclined to flower themselves to death but *C. grandiflora* is the worst offender, for which reason it has sometimes been referred to as a biennial. But it is a true perennial and will live for many years in a soil that is well drained and not too rich.

C. verticillata, quite a different plant and less well known, is extremely decorative. It grows about 2 feet high and has very small narrow almost fern-like leaves. The yellow flowers are also quite small but very freely produced in midsummer.

All these can be increased by division in the spring and also by seed sown in spring, though seedlings may prove a little variable.

The annual coreopsis are mostly hybrids and are often listed as calliopsis which, botanically, is an obsolete name. They vary in height from 1 to 3 feet and have flowers similar to those of *C. lanceolata* but in a variety of combinations of yellow and crimson. They are exceedingly showy plants both for the border and for cutting. Seed should be sown, in March, April, May or September, where the plants are to flower and the seedlings thinned to at least 9 inches apart.

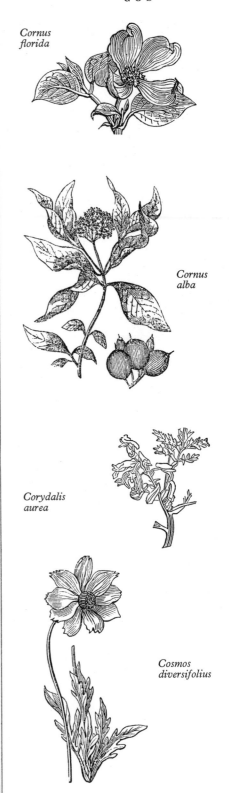

*Cornus
florida*

*Cornus
alba*

*Corydalis
aurea*

*Cosmos
diversifolius*

CORNUS   *(Dogwood)*

This is a big family of shrubs or small trees some of which are among the most beautiful and the most exclusive that can be cultivated in the open in this country, while others are little better than weeds. One needs, therefore, to be careful when making a selection of dogwoods.

The finest of the small trees are to be found among the American and Asiatic species such as *C. florida, C. Kousa, C. Nuttallii* and *C. capitata.* The last is tender and only suitable for the mildest places. The other three are also slightly suspect but are really much hardier and I have seen them thriving in quite cold gardens. Their young spring growth is apt to be cut by late frosts and this retards their growth and their flowering. Their true flowers are quite insignificant but they are surrounded by large and very showy petal-like bracts, usually white or ivory but a delightfully soft pink in *C. florida rubra.* All flower in spring.

Much easier to grow and a very useful garden shrub is *Cornus alba Spaethii*, a form of a wild British dogwood which is, therefore, perfectly hardy. A big bush with reddish stems and handsomely yellow-variegated leaves, I regard it as one of the ten or twelve best variegated shrubs and it has the added advantage that it will grow almost anywhere.

All these can be increased by cuttings of firm young wood in the autumn or by layering in early summer. The species (but not *C. alba Spaethii*) can also be raised from seed sown in a greenhouse or frame in spring.

CORYDALIS   *(Yellow Fumitory)*

The most familiar corydalis is *C. lutea*, a pretty perennial with pale green, fern-like leaves and sprays of small yellow flowers carried most of the summer. Growing about a foot high, it is often to be seen on the crumbling walls of old cottages and is a useful plant for such stony places, though rather a menace in the rock garden because of its tendency to seed itself everywhere. It is perfectly hardy and likes dry, well-drained places and poor soils. It can be increased in the spring, either by division or by seed. There are also other and choicer (but more difficult) kinds of which one of the best is *C. cheilanthifolia*, also with yellow flowers but a far less invasive habit.

COSMOS   *(Purple Mexican Aster)*

The cosmos commonly grown in gardens is *C. bipinnatus*, a familiar plant in late summer and early autumn, when its flat, broad-petalled daisy-flowers in various shades of pink, rose and wine red, as well as white, are at their best. Its tall masses of ferny foliage are also decorative but care must be taken not to grow this plant in too rich and moist a soil or it may be all foliage and no flowers.

It is a half-hardy annual, seed of which should be germinated in a warm greenhouse in February or early March. Prick off the seedlings and harden them off for planting out in late May or

41

*Cotinus
Coggygria*

*Cotoneaster
microphylla*

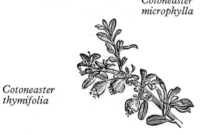

*Cotoneaster
thymifolia*

*Cotoneaster
frigida*

early June in a sunny place. Seed should be purchased from a reliable source as some strains do not flower at all well or start to flower so late that they are of little use.

COTINUS *(Wig Tree or Smoke Plant)*

Closely related to the sumach (rhus), *Cotinus Coggygria* is an excellent small tree or bush, up to 10 or 15 feet tall. It is often known as *Rhus Cotinus*. In July and August it is covered with curious 'flowers' made up of a large number of silk-like hairs in a tangled mass, at first a pale pinkish brown in colour, later turning grey (hence the popular names). The leaves take on magnificent autumn colourings before they fall in November. The variety *purpureus* (or *atropurpureus*) has purple leaves and purplish hairs. Another species, *C. americanus*, grows eventually to 20 feet and is worth having for its intense autumn colouring.

All these shrubs grow readily in any ordinary soil and open position and can be increased by cuttings of well ripened shoots inserted in sandy soil in autumn.

COTONEASTER

One of the great families of berry bearing shrubs and small trees, rivalling berberis in its importance for garden decoration. There are so many excellent species that it is difficult to confine selection to a mere eight or ten, but the following are, in my view, as good as any for general planting.

C. horizontalis is indispensable and unique because its rigid, fishbone-like branches will mould themselves to any surface against which they are planted. Placed alongside a rock they will throw themselves over it, near a wall they will ascend it without either clinging to it or requiring any support. The small neat leaves fall off in winter, when the scarlet berries set closely to the branches make a splendid display.

Closely allied to this but more rounded in habit and with narrower, evergreen leaves and deeper coloured, almost crimson berries, is *C. microphylla*. It is a grand shrub which is never seen to better advantage than when ascending (or descending) a wall.

Like miniature versions of the last, but deciduous, are *C. adpressa* and *C. congesta*, excellent dwarf shrubs for the rock garden.

C. conspicua decora has stiff spreading horizontal branches rather like *C. horizontalis*, but producing larger and more showy white flowers in May and crops of larger, scarlet berries in autumn. It is in the first rank of berry bearing shrubs.

Of the taller species the best appear to me to be *C. Franchetii*, *C. frigida*, *C. Dielsiana*, *C. Henryana*, *C. salicifolia*, *C. Simonsii* and *C. Wardii*. If I had to reduce this list to two they would be *C. frigida*, because it will make a small and shapely tree carrying great crops of crimson berries with unfailing regularity, and *C. Wardii* because it is a most elegant evergreen shrub eventually 8 or 10 feet in height with neat clusters of orange-red berries which are usually held well into the winter.

42

All are completely hardy and will thrive in any ordinary soil and open position. They can all be raised from seed sown in spring and most can also be raised from cuttings of firm young shoots in a frame in July.

CRATAEGUS *(Thorn, Quick)*

Another big family of shrubs or small trees (mostly the latter), many notable for their fruits. The common thorn or quick, *C. monogyna*, used for farm hedges, is hardly worth planting in the garden except in its double-flowered forms, one of which has pink and the other crimson flowers. These make shapely small trees suitable for gardens of moderate size, and flower very freely in May, but as their flowers are sterile, they are never followed by berries. They must therefore be increased by grafting in spring on to stocks of common thorn.

The famous Glastonbury thorn, another variety of the common thorn, has ordinary single white flowers. It is remarkable for the fact that it often produces some leaves and flowers in mid-winter. Its name is *C. monogyna biflora*.

The cockspur thorn, *C. Crus-galli*, notable for its very long and rigid thorns, is a good small tree with plentiful white flowers in May, good autumn foliage colour and handsome, deep red fruits.

Two other useful kinds are *C. Carrierei* and *C. prunifolia*, both small trees with handsome foliage and typical scarlet fruits. Those of *C. Carrierei* remain for a long time untouched by birds.

All are completely hardy and unfastidious. The species can be raised from seed sown outdoors in March. The varieties must be grafted on to seedling stocks.

CRINUM

These beautiful, lily-like plants suffer from the drawback of being on the border-line of tenderness. In warm and sheltered places they can be grown outdoors but an unusually severe winter may kill them. Probably the two hardiest kinds, and certainly the two most commonly seen, are *Crinum longifolium* (also known as *C. capense*) and *C. Powellii*. The first has white or pale pink trumpet shaped flowers, carried in crowded clusters on stout, 3–foot stems in August. *C. Powellii*, otherwise similar, has even larger flowers of a warmer pink.

They make very large bulbs which should be planted so that their necks are just out of the ground, in fairly rich but well-drained soils and warm sunny places. The foot of a south wall suits them well provided they are well watered in summer. They should be covered with a little dry straw or bracken in winter. Planting time is October and old clusters of bulbs can then be divided.

CROCUS

In addition to the well-known spring flowering crocuses in shades of mauve, lilac, purple and yellow, as well as white, there

Cotoneaster rotundifolia

Crataegus Crus-galli

Crataegus prunifolia

Crinum amabile

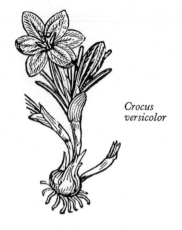

*Crocus
versicolor*

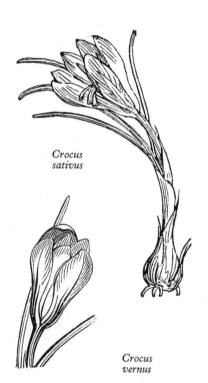

*Crocus
sativus*

*Crocus
vernus*

*Cyclamen
coum*

are a number of beautiful autumn and winter-flowering kinds which need a little more care in cultivation. These include *Crocus speciosus* with large violet-blue or white flowers in October or November; *C. zonatus* with lilac and yellow flowers at the same season; *C. chrysanthus*, which produces its yellow flowers in January or February; *C. Imperati*, usually January flowering and a very fine species, fawn without and violet within; *C. Sieberi*, pale-lilac, February flowering; *C. susianus*, golden yellow, either February or early March flowering; *C. versicolor*, which is variously striped purple on white; and *C. Tomasinianus*, with clear lavender flowers in February. The common, large flowered spring crocuses, hybrids sometimes referred to as Dutch crocuses, are available in mixed colours or in separate colours, sometimes under fancy names such as King of the Purples, Striped Beauty, etc.

The species, especially those that flower in autumn or winter, are really most at home in the rock garden though they can be grown in ordinary beds and borders provided the soil is fairly gritty and well drained. The common hybrids thrive in practically any soil. All like sunny places though they will also grow in the shade provided it is not too dense.

Planting time for autumn-flowering species is July or early August, for winter and spring kinds, September or October. The corms should be covered with 2 or 3 inches of soil and thereafter will require little attention beyond weeding. They should not be disturbed until they become so overcrowded that there is a falling off in the number and quality of their flowers. Then they can be lifted in July, divided into single corms and replanted.

CYCLAMEN *(Sowbread)*

These can conveniently be considered in two groups, for the varieties of *Cyclamen persicum* are greenhouse plants whereas most of the others are hardy plants to be grown outdoors. All make rather large tubers which have the peculiarity of growing either on the surface of the soil or just beneath it.

The greenhouse cyclamen are usually raised from seed sown in August in an unheated greenhouse. Germination is rather irregular and the seedlings are pricked off, a few at a time, into boxes of John Innes compost. When they begin to fill these comfortably they are potted singly, first into 3-inch pots, later into 4-inch, and finally into 5- or 6-inch pots, in which they will flower. John Innes potting compost can be used throughout.

The seedlings should be given greenhouse treatment until May or June of their second year. In winter they will need an average temperature of about 50°. In summer no artificial heat will be needed, but the glass should be lightly shaded and ventilation given freely. The seedlings should reach their flowering pots about 10 months after sowing. They will start flowering about November and continue most of the winter. After flowering the water supply can be gradually reduced to allow foliage to die down and the plants to rest. From the end of May until August they are best removed to a shady frame where they will

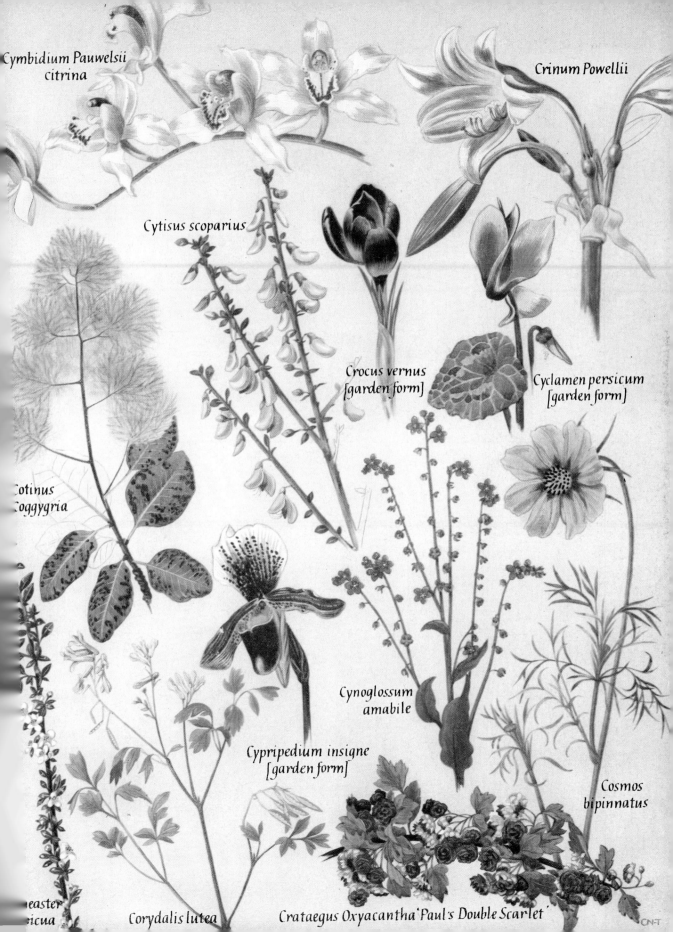

Cymbidium Pauwelsii
citrina

Crinum Powellii

Cytisus scoparius

Crocus vernus
[garden form]

Cyclamen persicum
[garden form]

Cotinus
Coggygria

Cynoglossum
amabile

Cosmos
bipinnatus

Cypripedium insigne
[garden form]

...easter
...icua

Corydalis lutea

Crataegus Oxyacantha 'Paul's Double Scarlet'

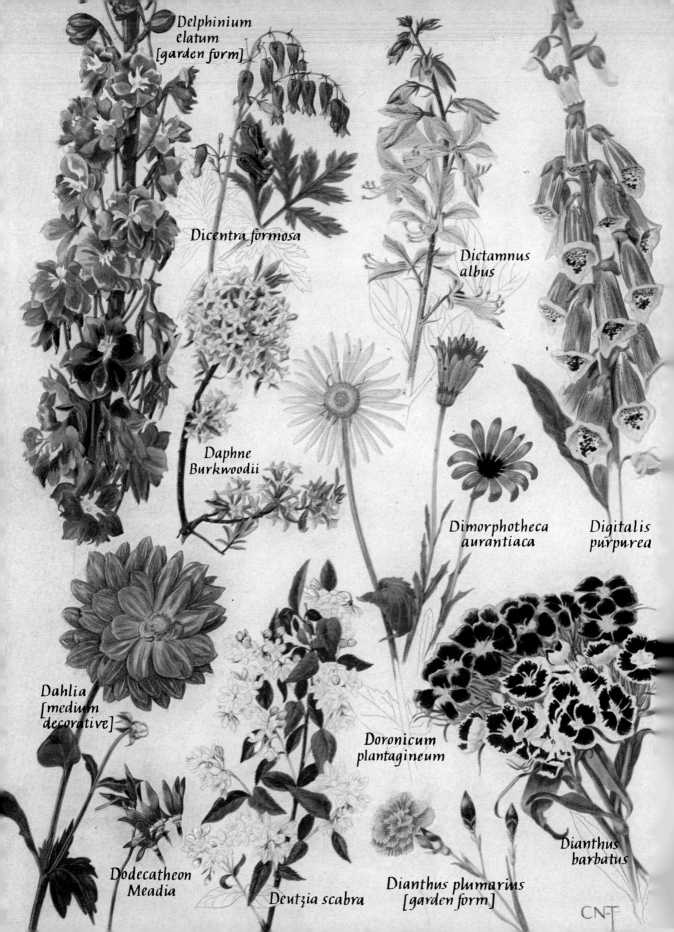

Delphinium
elatum
[garden form]

Dicentra formosa

Dictamnus
albus

Daphne
Burkwoodii

Dimorphotheca
aurantiaca

Digitalis
purpurea

Dahlia
[medium
decorative]

Doronicum
plantagineum

Dianthus
barbatus

Dodecatheon
Meadia

Deutzia scabra

Dianthus plumarius
[garden form]

CN-F

need little attention. In mid-August they can be repotted and watered more freely, and about a month later should be returned to the greenhouse where they will flower again in the winter. The circular tubers should be kept sitting just on top of the soil and must never be buried when repotting.

The hardy cyclamen have smaller flowers and vary in their time of flowering. *Cyclamen coum* produces small crimson flowers in February and March; *C. europaeum*, deep red blooms in August; *C. neapolitanum*, bright pink or white flowers in September.

All like cool, leafy soils in the rock garden, at the edge of shrubberies or in shady beds and borders. They like a certain amount of shade and resent root disturbance. Once established they should be left severely alone except for hand weeding. Start with small plants in pots, which can be put in at practically any time of the year, though spring is probably best. The tubers should be just covered with soil.

All hardy cyclamen can be raised from seed sown in a frame or cool greenhouse in spring.

CYMBIDIUM

These fine orchids are beautiful and comparatively easy to grow. They produce their long arching sprays of butterfly-like flowers in winter in a great variety of unusual colours including shades of green, amber, honey, bronze, buff, crimson and maroon. They last a very long time when cut and are invaluable for decoration. Cymbidiums are epiphytes which means that they obtain much of their food from the air. They are grown in a mixture of loam, sphagnum moss, osmunda fibre and decaying leaves, one recommended mixture being 3 parts of good fibrous loam, 1 part of sphagnum moss, 2 parts of osmunda fibre and 1 part of old, partly decayed oak or beech leaves. Plants should be repotted after flowering (usually in March), and it is usually sufficient to repot them every second year. They do not require high temperatures but should be kept at around 50° in winter and 60° in summer, with permanent shading from April to September. Syringe frequently with clear water in summer to maintain a moist atmosphere, but keep a little drier in early autumn when the bulb-like growths (correctly known as pseudo-bulbs) are ripening. Cymbidiums should be ventilated freely in favourable weather. They can be increased by careful division at potting time.

CYNOGLOSSUM *(Hound's Tongue)*

There are annuals, biennials and perennials in this genus and on the whole they are not, perhaps, a particularly distinguished lot apart from *Cynoglossum amabile*, a hardy plant, usually treated as an annual, which is notable for its brilliantly blue flowers. It is a rather sprawling plant, about 2 feet in height, like a coarse and large forget-me-not. Seed can be sown in a greenhouse or frame in March, and the seedlings planted out in May, to flower in July and August. Alternatively seed can be sown outdoors in

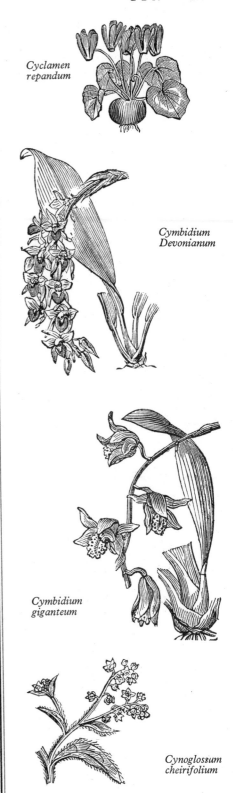

Cyclamen repandum

Cymbidium Devonianum

Cymbidium giganteum

Cynoglossum cheirifolium

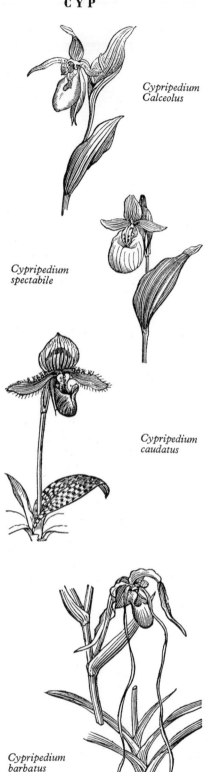

Cypripedium Calceolus

Cypripedium spectabile

Cypripedium caudatus

Cypripedium barbatus

late April where the plants are to flower, when the flowering season will be in August and September. This cynoglossum likes sunny places but is not particular about soil.

CYPRIPEDIUM (Lady's Slipper)

The cypripediums, unlike many orchids, do not grow perched up in trees, getting most of their food from the air, but in soil, with a more or less normal root system. Partly for this reason and partly because several kinds of cypripedium can be grown with little or no heat, they are among the best orchids with which an amateur can start.

Several are sufficiently hardy to be grown outdoors. Two of the best of these are *Cypripedium spectabile* which has rose-pink and white flowers, and *C. Calceolus*, with yellow and purple flowers. *C. pubescens*, rather like the last named, has larger flowers. All flower in late spring or early summer and are happiest in cool, rather moist leafy or peaty soils and partly shaded positions.

Of the greenhouse kinds easily the most popular is *C. insigne*, with green and chestnut coloured flowers, a fine and easily grown plant which has given rise to a great number of varieties and hybrids, among the best orchids for the amateur.

Compost for these greenhouse cypripediums consists of 2 parts of good medium loam, 1 part of sphagnum moss chopped fairly finely and 1 part of osmunda fibre well pulled apart. A little coarse silver sand should be added and a sprinkling of hoof and horn meal. Cypripediums mostly flower in the winter and should be repotted in spring when the flowers have faded. They have no marked resting period and must be watered all the year but much less frequently in autumn and winter than in spring and summer. They should be syringed frequently in warm weather and be shaded from hot sunshine.

All can be increased by careful division of the roots in spring. The name Lady's slipper refers to the conspicuous pouch, a feature of the flower of all species.

CYTISUS (Broom)

The brooms are among the most showy of spring flowering shrubs. Some of the best are varieties or hybrids of *Cytisus scoparius*, a tall, loose growing shrub with whippy, green branches and showy yellow flowers in May. The varieties and hybrids have flowers of primrose, deeper yellow, crimson, pink and various combinations of these.

There is a fine early flowering pale yellow broom, *C. praecox*, at its best in April; a tall and very graceful white kind named *C. albus*; the more or less prostrate spreading *C. Ardoinii* with yellow flowers; and *C. purpureus*, slightly taller but still spreading, with pale purplish-pink flowers. Very handsome in appearance but slightly less hardy is *C. Battandieri*, with comparatively large, silvery leaves and cylindrical clusters of bright yellow flowers in June. It makes a big, rather sprawling, loose habited shrub and is worthy of a warm and sheltered place.

All these delight in sunny places and rather poor, well-drained soils. They dislike root disturbance and should be raised in pots and transplanted from these to the open ground with as little injury to the roots as possible. They can be planted at any time from November to March inclusive.

They are rather susceptible to wind damage and in exposed places should be securely staked. All can be raised very readily from seed sown in spring in greenhouse or frame or even in the open ground, but seedlings of the hybrids and selected garden forms do not usually come quite true to type and where an exact reproduction of these is required, they must either be grafted (seedling laburnum is often used as a stock) or be raised from cuttings. This is not very easy but it can be done if the cuttings are prepared in August from firm young growths pulled off with a heel of older wood. These should be inserted in very sandy soil in a close frame.

Brooms do not normally require any pruning but if bushes become too big or grow straggly they can be trimmed over lightly immediately after flowering.

DAHLIA

The dahlias grown in gardens are complex, man-made hybrids, painstakingly developed for more than a hundred years. As a result, an extraordinary variety of flower shapes has been produced and for convenience these have been grouped in a classification devised by the National Dahlia Society and accepted by all dahlia growers. Full details are obtainable from the N.D.S. but for ordinary garden purposes it is only necessary to know its broad outlines. These consist of a number of groups such as decorative dahlias with double flowers composed of fairly broad petals; cactus dahlias with double flowers in which each petal is rolled downwards (in the most perfect cactus varieties the petal looks like a curved quill); show dahlias, with almost globular flowers as big as cricket balls and composed of short, almost tubular petals set with almost the precision of a honeycomb; pompon dahlias closely resembling the last but with much smaller flowers; collerette dahlias having single flowers with an extra ring of short petals, usually in a contrasting colour, around the disk-like centre; anemone-centred varieties, with a single row of large outer petals with a cushion-like centre of much shorter petals; true single-flowered varieties, and bedding dahlias which may be either single or double-flowered but are always quite dwarf, usually not above 2 feet in height.

All are grown in the same way except for minor variations necessitated by their height or the purpose for which they are required. All are half-hardy, i.e. they can be grown outdoors in summer but must be protected in winter, and all have tuberous roots. They can be increased either by carefully dividing the roots in spring or by taking cuttings of the young shoots as they appear in spring. The first method is simple and very effective but will not produce a great number of plants as each division must have a piece of the main crown of the plant, i.e. the hard part where stems and roots join. Cuttings enable a

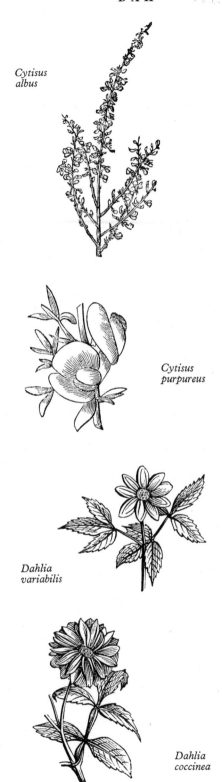

Cytisus albus

Cytisus purpureus

Dahlia variabilis

Dahlia coccinea

*Dahlia
(cactus)*

*Daphne
Genkwa*

*Daphne
collina*

*Daphne
Mezereum*

variety to be multiplied quickly but they must be rooted in a warm greenhouse and then hardened off.

When the cuttings are rooted they are potted singly in good soil (John Innes potting compost No. 1 will do well) and are grown on, first in the greenhouse and later in a frame in which they can be hardened off ready for planting out early in June. Dahlias like a sunny place and a rich soil, well dug and manured. The taller varieties should be staked securely for their stems are heavy and brittle. They like plenty of water. To obtain large flowers the flower buds should be restricted to one per stem.

In the autumn the top growth will be killed by frost. Then the roots should be lifted carefully and stored in a dry, fairly cool but frost-proof place until it is time either to start them into growth for cuttings or to divide and replant them outdoors, which should be done between mid-April and mid-May.

DAPHNE

Many of these beautiful shrubs are extremely sweetly scented. *Daphne Mezereum*, one of the earliest to flower, is deciduous and the purple or white flowers are produced in February or March along the bare stems. It grows about 4 feet high, is a little stiff and ungainly in habit and has a habit of dying unexpectedly without apparent cause, yet despite these defects it is a very desirable shrub because of its earliness and its fragrance.

D. Cneorum, a much smaller and neater evergreen, about a foot in height, bearing neat clusters of pink, fragrant flowers in May, is a good shrub for the rock garden in a sunny place and well-drained rather peaty soil.

Another good kind for the rock garden is *D. Blagayana*, prostrate, with clusters of very fragrant, creamy white flowers in May. It likes stony soils and it is a good plan to place small stones on its sprawling stems from time to time to hold them to the ground. In some ways the best of all is *D. Burkwoodii*, also known as *D. Somerset*, a neat bush about 3 feet high, semi-evergreen, with clusters of fragrant pink flowers in May and June. Both this and the purple flowered *D. collina* like sunny places.

D. odora is evergreen and 2 feet in height. Its purplish-rose flowers appear even earlier than those of *D. Mezereum* and it is desirable to give it a rather sheltered place. As its name implies it is sweetly scented. There are two forms, one with plain green leaves, the other margined with yellow.

Daphne Burkwoodii, *D. Cneorum* and *D. odora* can be increased by July cuttings of firm young growth rooted in a frame. *D. Mezereum* is best raised from seed. *D. Blagayana* usually layers itself and these rooted shoots can be detached in autumn.

DELPHINIUM *(Larkspur)*

Though strictly speaking 'delphinium' is simply the botanical name for the group of plants which should popularly be known as larkspurs, in practice gardeners nearly always mean the annual *Delphinium Ajacis* when they refer to larkspurs and they call the perennial kinds delphiniums. This is a very useful diff-

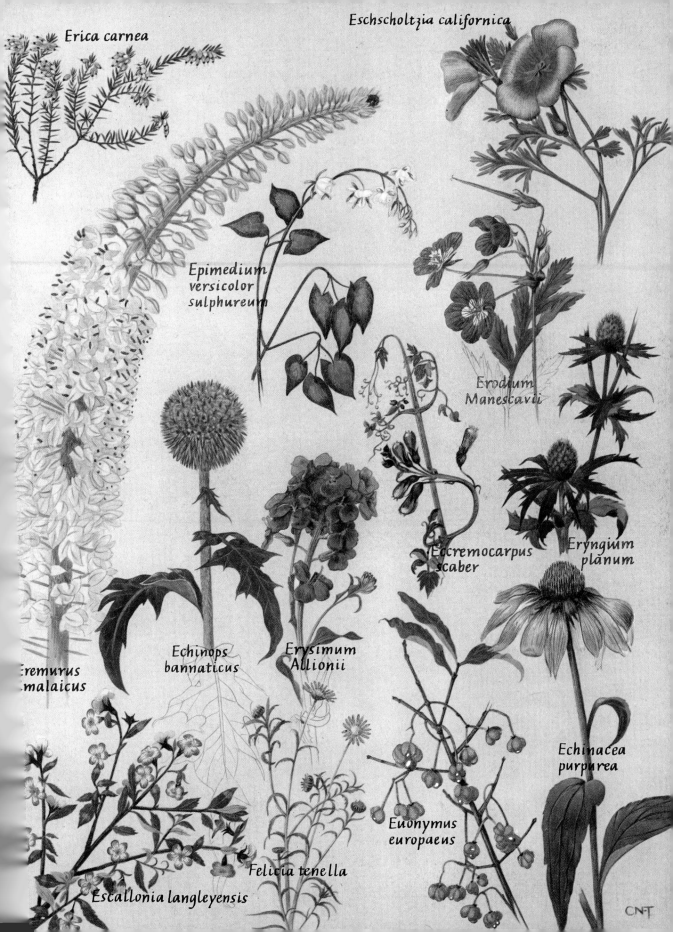

Erica carnea

Eschscholtzia californica

Epimedium
versicolor
sulphureum

Erodium
Manescavii

Eccremocarpus
scaber

Eryngium
planum

Eremurus
himalaicus

Echinops
bannaticus

Erysimum
Allionii

Echinacea
purpurea

Euonymus
europaeus

Felicia tenella

Escallonia langleyensis

CNT

Forsythia intermedia
spectabilis

Gazania
[garden forms]

Garrya
elliptica

Galanthus
nivalis

Geranium
grandiflorum

Gaillardia
aristata
[garden form]

Genista
aethnensis

Gentia
septemf

Fritillaria
gracilis

Freesia
refracta
[garden
form]

Fuchsia
'Royal Purple'

Galega
officinalis

Gardenia
jasminoides

Delphinium grandiflorum

Delphinium elatum

erentiation to remember for the annual and perennial kinds need quite different treatment.

The annuals are renewed from seed every year and the finest results are obtained by sowing this in September where the plants are to flower the following summer. Rather smaller plants and later flowers can be obtained by sowing in March or April, also in the open ground. Seedlings should be thinned to 9 or 12 inches. The tall, narrow spikes of bloom are very decorative and pink and white varieties are available as well as several shades of blue, lavender and violet. All are excellent for cutting as well as for garden display.

The perennials flower in June and July, sometimes giving a second display of smaller spikes in August or September, and seedlings usually flower in August in their first year. They may be considered in two groups, the tall 'elatum' varieties, with large spikes of bloom, and the shorter 'belladonna' varieties with small spikes or loose sprays of flowers. All like rather rich, well-drained soils and sunny positions. They may be planted in early autumn on the lighter soils but on heavier soils it is better to plant in March or early April. The large-flowered varieties require staking, preferably one stake to every flower spike, but the belladonna varieties can usually be grown without stakes or at most with a few brushy hazel branches for support.

Delphiniums can be increased either by careful division of the roots in spring, or by cuttings taken at the same season, prepared from young shoots 5 or 6 inches long, cut off close to the crown of the plant and inserted in sandy soil in a frame. The rooted cuttings can be planted out in late May or June.

The elatum delphiniums can also be raised from seed as soon as ripe in August or the following March. Sow in a frame or greenhouse and keep slugs away. The seedlings should be pricked off as soon as they can be handled and should be planted out in late May or early June. Most will flower the same year but there is usually a good deal of variation in the colour and habit of seedlings. However, certain American and English strains come remarkably true from seed.

DEUTZIA

The deutzias suffer from having no popular name and a botanical name that is not easy to remember. If it were not for this they could be as familiar as spiraeas or mock oranges, for they are equally decorative and useful shrubs. All have an erect habit of growth and attractive flowers in dense sprays at the ends of the branches. All are white or are flushed with pink or purple and all flower in June or July. Most of those grown in gardens are either varieties or hybrids of *Deutzia scabra* which is 7 or 8 feet in height and has white flowers. It has several double-flowered varieties one, Pride of Rochester, being suffused with purple and another, *candidissima*, being pure white. A fine rose pink hybrid is Mont Rose, while Avalanche has large white flowers. *D. gracilis* flowers earlier than most, is less tall and is frequently grown as a greenhouse pot plant.

Deutzia scabra

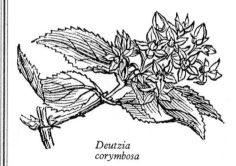

Deutzia corymbosa

D

49

Dianthus chinensis

Dianthus deltoides

Dianthus caesius

Dianthus alpinus

They all like sunny places but are not particular about soil. Old flowering stems can be cut out after flowering, if desired, but deutzias will grow quite happily without any pruning. They can be increased by cuttings of well-ripened young growth in early autumn.

DIANTHUS *(Carnation, Pink, Sweet William)*

This is one of the great garden families for in addition to numerous wild species suitable for the rock garden, it contains all those lovely summer blooming perennials familiarly referred to as pinks, as well as all the carnations both border and perpetual.

Border carnations are hardy and are grown outdoors, whereas perpetual flowering carnations are a little tender and are grown in greenhouses. Another difference is that border carnations flower once only in June or early July whereas, if carefully managed, perpetual carnations will flower throughout the year.

Most pinks derived from *Dianthus plumarius* flower in June but *Dianthus Allwoodii* hybrids have a longer flowering season, some continuing most of the summer.

All carnations like rather rich, loamy soils preferably containing a little lime. The perpetual flowering varieties may be grown in John Innes potting compost but the loam should be just a little heavier and richer than usual.

Perpetual carnations are raised from cuttings taken between November and March and inserted in pure silver sand or very sandy soil in a close frame at a temperature of about 60°. When rooted they are potted singly and moved on to larger pots as they fill the smaller sizes with roots, until they reach the 6- or 7-inch pots in which they will flower. The growing tips of the young plants are pinched out twice, first when they have seven pairs of leaves and again when the side shoots formed after the first stopping have made about seven pairs of leaves each. Plants can be grown in a deep frame from June to September but after that are better in a greenhouse. They do not need much heat but like an average temperature around 55°. As flower stems lengthen they will need careful staking. For best results the flowers are restricted to one per stem, other buds being removed at an early stage. It is wise to renew stock from cuttings every second or third year.

Border carnations are increased by layers pegged down in July. These should be rooted by September and can be severed from the parent plants, lifted and replanted. They like sunny open places and should be spaced about 18 inches apart. They need not be pinched like perpetual carnations and as they are not so tall, will need less elaborate staking. To get large blooms, restrict the flowers to one per stem but this is not necessary for garden display. Border carnations are classified according to colour, markings and perfume. Those known as cloves have a particularly rich perfume. Fancy carnations have markings of one colour, usually pink, red, crimson or lavender, on a ground of another colour. Self carnations are of one colour throughout. Picotees have a ground of one colour with a narrow margin to each petal of another colour. Bizarres and flakes have heavier and more blotched markings than the fancies.

Pinks are raised from cuttings taken in June or July and rooted in sandy soil outdoors or in a frame. They like open places, are not fussy about soil but appreciate good drainage.

The dianthus species cover a wide range from the cushion forming *Dianthus neglectus*, and trailing *D. deltoides*, to the erect, 2–foot high *D. superbus* with elegantly fringed flowers. They are plants for sunny places and light, well-drained soils. Many do well on walls or in rock gardens and most can be raised from seed sown in a greenhouse or frame in spring. Some can be carefully divided in spring when being transplanted.

Some dianthus are annuals or biennials, or are treated as such. *D. chinensis* and its variety *D. Heddewigii*, examples of the former, are grown as half-hardy annuals, seed being sown in a warm greenhouse in January or February. Seedlings are pricked off into boxes, carefully hardened off and planted out in May in a sunny place.

The Sweet William (*D. barbatus*) is usually grown as a biennial, seed being sown outdoors in May for flowering the following year. Seedlings should be moved to a nursery bed when they can be handled conveniently and finally removed to their flowering beds in September or October. At their best in June, they grow about 2 feet high and have large, flattish heads of brightly coloured flowers, usually pink, scarlet or crimson and white.

DICENTRA *(Bleeding Heart)*

Exceptionally graceful, hardy, June and July flowering perennials which will thrive in partially shaded positions. The three kinds commonly grown are *Dicentra eximia*, about a foot in height, with small carmine flowers; *D. formosa*, taller but otherwise similar; and *D. spectabilis*, at least 2 feet high, with larger pink and white flowers. All have decorative light green, ferny foliage. They can be grown in ordinary soil and are easily increased by division in spring or autumn. *D. spectabilis* is often grown as a pot plant for the unheated or slightly heated house.

DICTAMNUS *(Burning Bush, Gas Plant)*

The only species grown in gardens is *Dictamnus albus* (syn. *D. Fraxinella*). Called burning bush because it is said to give off an inflammable gas, which can be ignited on a warm day, it is a striking and decorative hardy perennial about 3 feet in height with spikes of purple or white flowers in summer. It likes cool shady places and ordinary soils and can be increased from seed or by dividing old roots in spring or autumn.

DIGITALIS *(Foxglove)*

The common foxglove of British hedgerows and woodlands is a biennial or short-lived perennial which, though hardly worth transplanting to the garden in its ordinary purple-flowered form, has given rise to a number of other forms, admirable for rough or shady places. These have larger flowers and the colour range

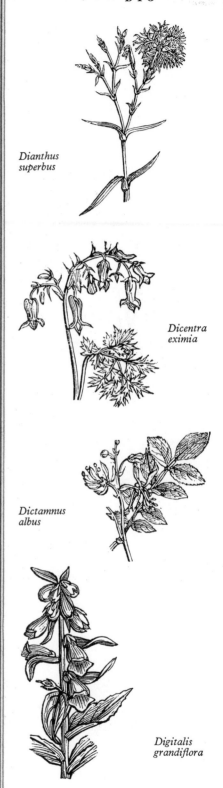

Dianthus superbus

Dicentra eximia

Dictamnus albus

Digitalis grandiflora

51

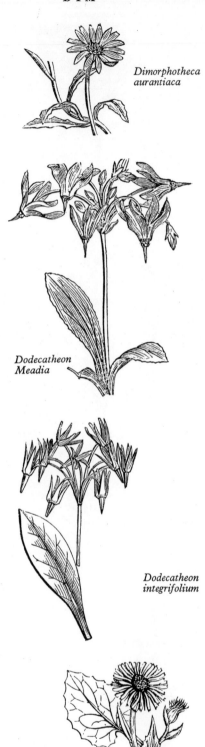

*Dimorphotheca
aurantiaca*

*Dodecatheon
Meadia*

*Dodecatheon
integrifolium*

*Doronicum
Pardalianches*

is from white and pale pink to crimson, some very beautifully netted with one shade on another. A recent development, known as the Excelsior strain, has flowers held almost horizontally all round the stem instead of drooping on one side only.

All these can be very easily raised from seed sown outdoors in May. The seedlings should be pricked off in a nursery bed, and moved from this in autumn to the place in which they are to flower. They look well among shrubs or in good drifts in thin woodland. There are also perennial species, such as *D. ambigua* with dull yellow flowers.

DIMORPHOTHECA *(Star of the Veldt)*

These are all sun-loving daisies best treated as annuals in this country. They are valuable in the garden because they bring to it a range of colours not commonly found in anything else—shades between orange and apricot, yellow and buff. All grow about 1 foot high and flower in summer according to the time at which they are sown. For the earliest flowers seed should be sown in a greenhouse or frame in March, the seedlings pricked off into boxes and hardened off for planting out in late May or early June. For later flowers seed can be sown outdoors in April or early May where the plants are to flower and the seedlings thinned to 9 inches apart. A position in full sun is essential as in shade the flowers do not open properly. They will grow in almost any soil but prefer that which is fairly light and well drained.

DODECATHEON *(Shooting Star, American Cowslip)*

The dodecatheons are extremely attractive plants for the bog garden. The flowers are not unlike small cyclamens carried on stiffly erect stems which may be anything from 12 to 18 inches in height. That most commonly grown in British gardens is *Dodecatheon Meadia* with rosy-purple or white flowers in May. It thrives best in a very moist place, alongside a pool or a slow moving stream, and it likes peaty soils, though there should be enough grit in them to allow moisture to keep moving freely through them. The best method of increase is by seed sown in spring in a greenhouse or frame in sandy peat.

DORONICUM *(Leopard's Bane)*

These are hardy herbaceous perennials, useful because they flower so early. The bright yellow daisies of the best kind, *Doronicum plantagineum*, are often out in April and are at their best in May. Each bloom is about 3 inches in diameter and as the flowers are carried on good 3-foot stems, they are excellent for cutting as well as for garden display. An improved variety known as *excelsum* or Harpur Crewe has even larger flowers. *D. Pardalianches* is a less showy, very hardy British species.

Doronicums are not at all fussy about soil, will succeed in full sun or partial shade and are readily increased by division in spring or autumn. I have seen them very happily naturalized in grass where they looked like yellow moon daisies.

ECCREMOCARPUS *(Chilean Glory Flower)*

Only one species, *Eccremocarpus scaber*, is grown in gardens. A slender climber with small, ferny leaves, it has tubular orange-red flowers in summer. It comes from Chile and is a little tender in Britain. For this reason, and also because it grows very rapidly from seed, it is often treated as an annual. However, it is a true perennial and it is worth a specially warm and sheltered place, for example, against a wall or fence facing south, for then it will go on from year to year and give a magnificent display. It will reach a height of about 12 feet and cover quite an area. Seed should be sown in a greenhouse either as soon as ripe or in March. Pot the seedlings singly and harden them off for planting out in late May. The plants climb by tendrils so should have some support to which these can cling.

Eccremocarpus scaber

ECHINACEA *(Purple Cone Flower)*

The only species of echinacea grown in gardens is the purple flowered *E. purpurea*. The flowers are like big daisies with a dark central disk in the manner of many rudbeckias (it is sometimes known as *Rudbeckia purpurea*.) The colour is unusual and difficult to describe, rather like the stains of purple plum juice, and is a useful addition to the border. It is a hardy herbaceous perennial easily grown in any fairly moist but reasonably porous soil and open position. It can be increased by division in spring or autumn. The varieties differ a little in the precise shade of their colour and also in height, which varies from 3 to 4 feet. One of the best is The King.

Echinacea purpurea

ECHINOPS *(Globe Thistle)*

The globe thistles are distinctly handsome and unusual hardy herbaceous plants. Their flower heads are almost perfect spheres made up of small, closely packed blue flowers which fall off to reveal a striking, spiky, metallic-blue seed head. They are a little coarse in leaf but that is their only fault. All are extremely hardy and easily grown in practically any soil. They like an open position and good drainage and can be increased very readily from seed or, more slowly, by careful division in spring of their long, thongy roots. A third alternative is to take root cuttings in winter and start these in a frame. The names of the various kinds seem to have become rather mixed in gardens and nurseries and that commonly offered as *Echinops Ritro* is not, apparently, that rather dwarf (1 to 2-foot) species but the much larger 5-foot, *E. sphaerocephalus*. Another attractive species often offered is *E. bannaticus*, about 3 feet tall.

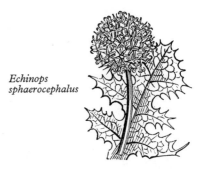

Echinops sphaerocephalus

EPIMEDIUM *(Barrenwort)*

The epimediums while not showy plants have the merit of attractive foliage which usually colours well in the autumn, small but dainty flowers like those of barberries, to which they are related, and an ability to thrive in quite dense shade. All are hardy herbaceous perennials of comparatively low growth

Epimedium pinnatum

53

Epimedium
alpinum

Eremurus
himalaicus

Erica
Tetralix

Erica
mediterranea

suitable for planting at the front of the border or as undercover beneath shrubs. The most common kind, *E. versicolor sulphureum*, has pale sulphur yellow flowers in spring. It can be easily increased by division. *E. alpinum* with dull red flowers, *E. pinnatum*, bright yellow and *E. niveum*, white are occasionally seen.

EREMURUS *(Fox-tail Lily)*

The fox-tail lilies are among the most handsome and imposing of all hardy herbaceous perennials but are not very easy to grow. Their fleshy roots spread out from a central crown like the spokes of a wheel and they do not much like being disturbed, let alone broken. Moreover the crowns themselves are a little tender, particularly when starting into growth in early spring and should be protected with small heaps of sharp ashes, coarse sand or dry bracken placed over them in the autumn and left until growth breaks through in the spring.

They like an open, not too dry soil and a sunny position. I have seen them doing well on chalk and also on a light fenland soil, so their range of tolerance in this respect is fairly great. The fleshy roots should be planted in September or October with as little injury as possible, spread out to their full extent in a wide, shallow hole. They do not need more than 4 inches of soil over them. Once established leave them undisturbed for as long as possible. Each year they will send up increasingly large clumps of strap-shaped leaves from which will be thrown up, in June or July, fine stiff stems terminated by huge spikes of white, pink, yellow or apricot flowers. There are many species and hybrids, among the best being *E. Bungei* with 4 or 5–foot spikes of maize yellow flowers; *E. himalaicus*, white, 5 feet; *E. Elwesii*, pink, 5 feet; *E. Olgae*, white, lightly striped with brown; and *E. robustus*, one of the tallest, its pale pink spikes often reaching 9 or 10 feet. The best method of increase is by seed sown as soon as ripe in September in sandy soil in a frame.

ERICA *(Heather, Heath)*

There are a great many different kinds of heather, most of them hardy but a few are either slightly tender and need sheltered places outdoors or are completely tender and must be grown in pots in a greenhouse. They like leafy or peaty soils and most dislike lime though a few, such as *Erica carnea* and *E. darleyensis*, will tolerate it in small quantities.

There are heathers to flower in practically every month of the year and heights vary from the completely prostrate *Calluna Vulgaris minima* to the 8 or 10 feet high *Erica arborea*. Colours range from white and palest pink to deep crimson.

One of the most useful is *E. carnea*, 9 to 12 inches high, compact and early flowering (February-March), with many varieties from white to deep carmine. It will stand some lime. *E. darleyensis* is similar but a little taller and even earlier flowering.

E. cinerea flowers in June and August, *E. vagans* from August to October, *E. tetralix* from June to October, *E. mediterranea* from February to March and *E. arborea* from March to April. There are different varieties of all these.

The wild heather of English commons is not an erica at all but a near relative, *Calluna vulgaris*. It also has numerous varieties and requires identical treatment.

The most popular greenhouse heathers are *E. gracilis* and *E. hyemalis*. They require frost protection only and in summer are best outdoors in a sheltered plunge bed. They need very careful watering at all times and should be grown in a lime-free, peaty compost.

All ericas can be increased by layering or by cuttings of young shoots in summer inserted in a frame.

ERODIUM   *(Heron's Bill)*

The erodiums are small rock garden plants, not notably showy but attractive in a quiet way, and good mat-forming plants some of which make excellent ground cover for bulbs. Very easily grown in almost any soil, they like open sunny places and can be quickly increased by division in spring or autumn. My own favourite is *Erodium chamaedryoides roseum* (often but, I think, erroneously, called *E. Reichardii roseum*) because it is so very neat, with small rounded leaves and the daintiest pale pink flowers scattered on it like confetti from spring to autumn. *E. guttatum* is about 6 inches in height with small clusters of bright pink flowers in June. *E. chrysanthum* has yellow flowers and particularly attractive silvery-grey leaves deeply cut into fine segments. *E. Manescavii* is one of the tallest of all, 1 to 1½ feet high with crude but effective rosy-purple flowers.

ERYNGIUM   *(Sea Holly)*

The eryngiums, hardy herbaceous perennials with stiff, rather spiny leaves, have teazle-like heads of flowers which can, if desired, be dried and kept for winter decorations. The flowers are mostly blue, sometimes an odd steely blue that is both unusual and attractive, but at least one, *Eryngium giganteum*, has bone-white flowers. It is larger than most, often 6 feet in height, and not a very reliable perennial in our damp, cold winters and is often treated as a biennial.

They all like light, sandy soils and are less permanent in those that are heavy and badly drained. The stout, thongy roots penetrate deeply into the ground, and they are not very easy to lift or divide. They can be increased quite readily from root cuttings taken in winter and started into growth in sandy soil in a frame. Seed also germinates readily in a frame or greenhouse in spring, and seedlings will flower in their second season.

One of the most reliable is *E. planum*. Individually its blue flower heads are rather small but they are produced in great umbers in fine branching sprays and are particularly good for tting. *E. amethystinum* is amethyst-blue, *E. Oliverianum* is a fine metallic blue and *E. Violetta* a most unusual violet with a flush of amethyst. All flower in July and are about 3 feet in height.

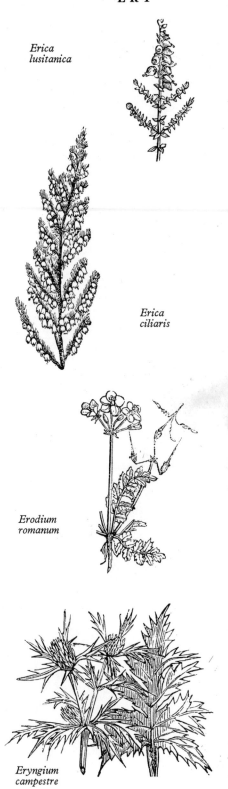

Erica lusitanica

Erica ciliaris

Erodium romanum

Eryngium campestre

*Erysimum
Perofskianum*

*Escallonia
macrantha*

*Escallonia
rubra*

*Eschscholtzia
californica*

ERYSIMUM *(Siberian Wallflower)*

This very popular plant is neither a wallflower nor a native of Siberia. Its proper name is *Erysimum Allionii* (not *Cheiranthus Allionii* as it usually appears in seed lists) and it is a native of California. It is one of the showiest plants that can be raised quickly and easily from seed to flower in late spring and early summer. Indeed its one fault is that it continues to produce its vivid orange, wallflower-like flowers for so long that when they do eventually finish, about midsummer, it is getting a little late to replace it with anything else. Seed should be sown outdoors in May the seedlings being transplanted in June to a nursery bed and removed to their flowering quarters in September or October. They should be planted 9 inches to 1 foot apart, preferably in bold masses so that they make a solid sheet of colour when in bloom. They are not at all fussy about soil but they do like sun. *E. Perofskianum* is a yellow or orange flowered annual up to 2 feet in height.

ESCALLONIA

These extremely attractive shrubs, nearly all evergreen, are not quite hardy enough for the coldest parts of the country. They are admirable seaside shrubs and do well in the south and west. Some of the hardiest kinds, such as *E. langleyensis* and *E. edinensis*, will also grow well in many other places if reasonably sheltered.

E. langleyensis, an outstandingly beautiful shrub, makes a big bush of arching branches with neat, glossy foliage and small rosy-carmine flowers all along the stems in June and July. Closely allied and very similar, but with pale pink flowers, is *E. edinensis*.

E. macrantha, stiffer in habit, has larger leaves, is more tender and, therefore, less generally useful.

There are also a number of hybrids such as C. F. Ball, a grand crimson with flowers larger than most; Slieve Donard, with rose-pink flowers and the arching habit of *E. langleyensis*, and Apple Blossom, pink and white, all good but generally less hardy than *E. langleyensis*.

All should be grown in sunny but sheltered positions. They can be grown against walls but this rather spoils their natural grace. I have not found them at all fussy about soil and they can be very easily increased by cuttings prepared from firm young shoots in July or August and rooted in a close frame or under a handlight.

ESCHSCHOLTZIA *(Californian Poppy)*

These are among the most cheerful and the most easily grown of hardy annuals. *E. californica* has finely divided almost fern-like, greyish-green leaves and poppy-like flowers, typically orange, but developed in gardens to include all shades from ivory white to crimson. They love dry sunny places and will often naturalize themselves in such places, coming up year after year from self-sown seed. Seed may be sown in March,

April, May or September where the plants are to flower, the seedlings being thinned to about 9 inches apart. Eschscholtzias grow about 1 foot high, have a sprawling but not untidy habit, and will continue to flower all the summer.

EUONYMUS *(Spindle Tree)*

A family of shrubs and small trees some of which are evergreen and some deciduous. The popular name, spindle tree, only belongs to the latter group, most of which have a rather angular habit and make open shrubs bearing small but brightly coloured fruits in autumn. The evergreen species are much denser in habit for which reason certain kinds are much planted as hedges. For this *Euonymus japonicus* and its numerous varieties are outstanding. The commonest form has dark green, glossy leaves and will grow to a height of 12 or 15 feet. It stands clipping well and thrives in seaside districts. The forms of *E. japonicus* mostly have variegated leaves and differ in the colour and distribution of the variegation, some being yellow, some silver, some margined with the variegation and others with a splash of variegation in the centre of each leaf.

Another good evergreen is *E. radicans*, a shrub which will climb when planted against a wall or, if placed in the open, will spread laterally and not grow above a couple of feet in height. Its leaves are smaller and lighter in colour than those of *E. japonicus* and like that species it has numerous variegated varieties.

Of the deciduous kinds two of the best known are the British spindle tree, *E. europaeus*, and *E. latifolius* which has larger leaves. The first has pink fruits which split open to reveal orange seeds. *E. latifolius* has scarlet fruits with similar seeds and its foliage colours well in the autumn. Even better for autumn colour is *E. alatus*, a shrub with curiously winged branches. Its leaves turn a magnificent crimson or ruby red just before they fall.

All the evergreen kinds can be increased by cuttings of firm young growth taken in early autumn and rooted in a frame. The deciduous kinds are readily raised from seed though, as seedlings may vary a little, specially desirable forms must be increased by cuttings as for the evergreens. None is particular regarding soil and the evergreens will tolerate some shade but the true spindle-trees prefer a sunny position.

FELICIA *(Blue Daisy, Blue Marguerite)*

The best felicia for gardens is *F. amelloides*, a pretty little sun-loving plant often known as *Agathaea coelestis*. Its small, blue daisy flowers are produced most of the summer. It makes a bushy plant 18 inches or more in height eventually, though as it is frequently grown as an annual and then does not have time to reach its full dimensions, it is commonly seen as a small plant 9 to 12 inches high. Not quite hardy enough to winter outdoors except in the mildest places, it can, if desired, be grown as a pot plant for the greenhouse where it is useful both for its long flowering season and its ability to survive with no more than frost

Euonymus japonicus

Euonymus latifolius

Euonymus europaeus

Felicia fragilis

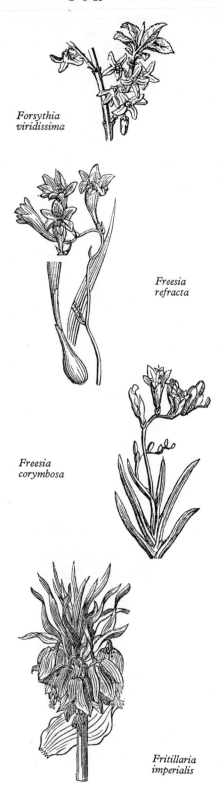

Forsythia
viridissima

Freesia
refracta

Freesia
corymbosa

Fritillaria
imperialis

protection. Seed provides the easiest means of increase and should be sown in a slightly heated greenhouse in February or March. *F. tenella* is an annual, 1 foot high, with similar flowers.

FORSYTHIA *(Golden Bells)*

Forsythias are among the best and most popular of early spring flowering shrubs. Their robustness, ease of culture and free flowering qualities make them general favourites. The best, judged solely on these qualifications, is *F. intermedia spectabilis*, of stiff but not ungainly habit, capable of reaching a height of 10 feet with corresponding spread, though it can be restricted without much difficulty. Its flowers are a particularly bright yellow. It is a pity that its undoubted merits have rather over-shadowed the less spectacular but more graceful *F. suspensa*. This has long, slender arching branches, nearly black in the variety named *atrocaulis*, and paler yellow flowers.

All bloom in March or early April and can be pruned, if desired, by cutting out the old flowering branches as soon as the flowers fade. They can be increased by cuttings of firm young stems taken in autumn and rooted in a frame or sheltered place outdoors.

They are not particular about soil and will tolerate some shade though they prefer an open position. *F. suspensa* can be trained against a fence or wall if desired.

FREESIA

Now that the colour range has been greatly increased and seed has been made available at a comparatively low cost, freesias are becoming very popular as fragrant winter-flowering plants for the cool greenhouse. They make small corms or bulbs and can be grown from these. Alternatively they can be raised from seed and, if this is sown in a warm greenhouse in February or March, the seedlings will flower the same year. They should be grown six or seven together in a 5-inch pot in John Innes compost. During the summer they will be quite happy in a frame as they are nearly hardy (freesias grow outdoors without protection in Cornwall). In autumn they should be returned to the greenhouse and given just sufficient heat to maintain a temperature around 50°. The rather thin flower stems will require some support. After flowering the water supply should be gradually reduced until by about June no water is given at all and the corms are allowed to rest for a few weeks. In late July or early August they can be shaken out of the soil, separated and repotted

Varieties are available in various shades of blue, lavender, mauve, yellow and red and there is also the old white *Freesia refracta alba* and a number of larger flowered white varieties

FRITILLARIA *(Fritillary, Snake's Head, Crown Im-perial)*

These are bulbous rooted plants with nodding, bell shaped flow-ers, but the numerous species differ greatly in stature and appearance. The two most useful in gardens are *Fritillaria*

Meleagris, an uncommon native of Britain which grows freely in some damp meadows near the Thames, and *F. imperialis*. *F. Meleagris* carries its purple flowers, chequered or veined with a lighter shade, in ones or twos on slender, foot high stems. An elegant but rather oddly coloured plant, it is at its best in April and May. It likes damp rich soils and, where conditions suit it, can be naturalized very effectively in grass. Rather similar but with brown and yellow chequering is *F. gracilis*.

F. imperialis is a stout plant with stiff, leafy stems 3 feet high, crowned in May by a complete circle of yellow or reddish flowers of considerable size. A most striking plant for the border, unfortunately it (and particularly its large bulb) has a most unpleasantly pungent smell. It will grow in any ordinary soil and sunny position.

Fritillary bulbs should be planted in September or October, covered with 2 or 3 inches of soil, which will mean taking out quite small holes for *F. Meleagris* and much bigger and deeper ones for *F. imperialis*. Space the former 6 inches and the latter 18 inches apart.

FUCHSIA

The fuchias are fine decorative shrubs just on the borderline of hardiness. Some of the larger-flowered kinds require greenhouse protection in winter, as they can survive little or no frost, while others, mainly those with rather smaller flowers, may be grown outdoors winter and summer in fairly mild or sheltered places. Fine fuchsia hedges are to be seen in some southern and western regions, particularly near the sea where fuchsias nearly always thrive. Even when severely damaged by frost they will usually send up fresh growth from ground level, but under such conditions they do not make the fine specimens found in milder places.

Apart from this difficulty of tenderness, all are very easily grown. They will thrive in most soils and, when grown in pots or tubs, are well suited by John Innes compost. They can be quickly and easily raised from cuttings of firm young shoots, taken at practically any time of year, inserted in sandy soil in a close frame. They do not mind a certain amount of shade though they will also thrive in full sun, and they are excellent town shrubs. No regular pruning is required but dead or injured growth should be removed each spring. In the greenhouse they should be given pots or tubs of ample size to contain their roots and should be watered freely in summer but sparingly in winter. Only enough heat to exclude frost will be required.

GAILLARDIA

Two distinct kinds of gaillardia are commonly grown in gardens, the one annual and the other perennial. The annuals are derived from *Gaillardia pulchella* and its variety *picta*, whereas the perennials are all varieties of *G. aristata*. All have daisy-like flowers mainly in shades of yellow and red, but those of the perennials are larger and more showy and they are altogether

Fritillaria Meleagris

Fuchsia magellanica Riccartonii

Fuchsia magellanica (garden form)

Fuchsia fulgens

*Gaillardia
bicolor*

*Galanthus
plicatus*

*Galanthus
nivalis*

*Galega officinalis
albiflora*

finer garden plants. Many are yellow with a broad central ring
of scarlet. Some are yellow throughout and some are a deep
orange or bronze-red. The perennials are about 2 feet in height
and the annuals are, in general, a few inches shorter.

Gaillardias are sun loving plants and they like well-drained
soils. All tend to have stems a little too weak for the size and
weight of their flowers and consequently benefit from some
support

Seed of the annuals may either be sown in a greenhouse or
frame in March or outdoors in April or May. Under glass the
seedlings must be pricked off into boxes and hardened off for
planting out 9 to 12 inches apart in May. In the open seedlings
may be thinned to 9 inches.

The perennials can also be raised from seed though the
seedlings are unlikely to flower until their second year. Alternatively, old plants can be divided in spring or young plants can be
raised from root cuttings taken in winter and started into growth
in sandy soil in a frame.

GALANTHUS *(Snowdrop)*

The common snowdrop, *Galanthus nivalis*, one of the loveliest
spring flowering bulbs, needs no description. There are, however,
others equally beautiful but less well known. Outstanding among
these are *G. byzantinus*, *G. Elwesii*, *G. Ikariae* and *G. plicatus*,
all rather larger than the common snowdrop, with broader
leaves, but otherwise having the same gracefully formed, nodding white and green flowers. All flower in late winter or early
spring. The double flowered form of *G. nivalis*, though less
dainty, is more effective in the mass.

All these are perfectly easy to grow in ordinary soil and cool
position. The common kind is admirable for naturalizing in
short grass in partially shaded positions, but the others are
better in the rock garden or border without the competition of
grass and weeds. The bulbs should be planted 4 inches deep
in early autumn. Old clumps of bulbs can be lifted and divided
in summer after the foliage has died down.

GALEGA *(Goat's Rue)*

The galegas, rather coarse and rampant hardy herbaceous perennials, attractive when carrying their abundant clusters of small,
pea-type flowers, will thrive in quite poor soils and rough places.
The best species is *Galega officinalis*, 3 or 4 feet high, carrying
its bluish mauve flowers from June to early August. It has several
good varieties such as *Hartlandii*, pale blue, and Lady Wilson,
pinkish lilac.

They will grow in practically any soil and an open or partially
shaded position. They can be planted in spring or autumn and
are readily increased by division of the roots at either season.

GARDENIA

The gardenia, an evergreen shrub, needs the protection of a
warm greenhouse. It is grown mainly for cutting as the waxy

white, heavily perfumed flowers are greatly prized as button-holes and for bouquets, shoulder sprays, etc. The kind usually cultivated is *Gardenia jasminoides* which needs an average winter temperature of about 55° (minimum 45°). In summer the temperature can rise a good deal higher provided the plants are freely watered, frequently syringed and lightly shaded. Much less water and overhead moisture is required in autumn and winter and the plants can be kept rather cool and a little on the dry side for a while to rest them. Successive batches can be started into growth from January to March to flower from March to June. This is done simply by raising the temperature a little and increasing the water supply. Gardenias can be increased by cuttings of young shoots in spring, rooted in sand in a propagating case, with a temperature of about 70°.

GARRYA *(Silk Tassel Bush)*

In Britain *Garrya elliptica* has no popular name but in America it is known as the silk tassel bush and this is so appropriate that I have used it in the hope that it may be adopted here. It is a fine evergreen shrub, dense and rounded in habit, perhaps as much as 12 feet high when fully grown and unrestricted, but usually seen at about two thirds that height. In mid-winter it produces slender grey-green catkins which gradually lengthen and, in the male form (there are two sexes in this plant) become about 8 inches long and have yellow stamens. The female form has shorter catkins and, of course, no stamens so is not quite as decorative.

A good and unusual shrub, it is worth a little special care. It should be given a sunny sheltered position, indeed I have seen it trained most effectively against a wall though this must have involved a good deal of work as it is naturally a very bushy plant. It appreciates a good but reasonably well-drained soil and does not require regular pruning. Propagation is by cuttings of firm young shoots taken in July or August, rooted in a propagating frame in a greenhouse.

GAZANIA

These are trailing perennials for warm sunny places, have large and very showy daisy flowers, usually in bright shades of orange or orange-red, often with a darker, almost black, zone. The flowers only open in the sun so it is useless to grow them in shady places.

They can be grown outdoors during summer, and in the milder parts of the country some will survive outdoors in winter, but usually it is best to give them frame protection from October to early May. They can be increased easily either from seed sown in a slightly heated greenhouse in spring or by cuttings of firm young shoots taken at almost any time in spring and summer, and rooted in sandy soil in a frame. Gazanias will grow in quite poor soils and like best those that are light and well drained. They are attractive for dry walls, rock gardens, the edges of borders, or summer bedding schemes.

61

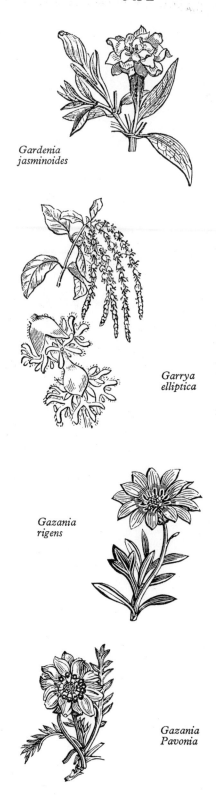

Gardenia jasminoides

Garrya elliptica

Gazania rigens

Gazania Pavonia

Genista
hispanica

Genista
lydia

Genista
sagittalis

Gentiana
septemfida

GENISTA (Broom)

The popular name 'broom' is shared by both genista and cytisus and there is some botanical confusion between the two genera. The fragrant genista of florists' shops, once known as *Genista fragrans*, is now named *Cytisus fragrans*, and other species have been similarly transferred.

All are sun-loving shrubs with yellow flowers and most are fully hardy. In general they are deciduous but their green stems give them some of the effect of evergreens. They do well in poor, rather dry, well-drained soils. They can all be raised very readily from seed sown in greenhouse or frame in spring, seedlings usually flowering in their second year.

Genista aethnensis is one of the largest, an almost tree-like shrub, 12 to 15 feet in height, with long, nearly pendent, whip-like stems wreathed throughout their length in July with the small yellow flowers.

Equally large but stiffer and more erect in habit are *G. cinerea* and *G. virgata*, both flowering in June and July.

At the other extreme are *G. lydia* and *G. tinctoria*, both almost prostrate, spreading shrubs suitable for the rock garden, the top of a dry wall or the front of a border. *G. lydia* has a particularly delightful habit, its arching shoots producing a wave-like effect. *G. tinctoria* has an attractive double-flowered form and *G. sagittalis* is an interesting but less showy species.

Another popular kind is *G. hispdnica*, often known as the Spanish gorse, a fine spring plant about 2 feet high, which might be described as a dwarf and very neat gorse. It will spread over a considerable area and flowers in May and June.

GENTIANA (Gentian)

The name gentian conjures up pictures of the most brilliantly blue flowers. This is true of some of the best species but by no means all gentians are of such pure colour, indeed some are not even blue at all. The family is a large one of great variety. *Gentiana verna*, a rare British native, no more than 3 inches high, produces its ultramarine blue flowers in spring. At the other extreme is *G. lutea*, a rather coarse plant, 5 or 6 feet high, bearing yellow flowers in early summer. It is not a particularly desirable garden plant.

Two of the most popular and beautiful are *G. acaulis* and *G. sino-ornata*. The first flowers in spring, the second in autumn. Both have large, trumpet shaped flowers, those of *G. acaulis* deep blue, those of *G. sino-ornata* a much lighter blue striped with white. *G. Farreri* is similar but more difficult to grow. Another of the same character is *G. Macaulayi*, a hybrid between *G. sino-ornata* and *G. Farreri* which has inherited the beauty of both its parents and is easier to grow than either of them.

Good summer flowering kinds are *G. septemfida*, *G. lagodechiana*, and *G. Freyniana*, all with compact clusters of purple flowers. They sprawl about, turning their shoots up to hold their flowers clear of the ground, but are never above 9 inches in height. Some authorities regard *G. lagodechiana* and *G. Frey-niana* as varieties of *G. septemfida*, a little more compact in growth or a few shades darker in colour. All three are easy.

Very different again is *G. asclepiadea*, often known as the willow gentian, presumably because of its gracefully arching habit. It makes slender, more or less erect stems, 18 inches high, carrying loose sprays of deep blue flowers, at their best about mid-summer. Unlike the preceding species, which are sun-lovers, it prefers cool, partially shaded places and may be naturalized in thin woodland.

All gentians like leafy or peaty soils well supplied with moisture in summer but not prone to waterlogging in winter. They are ideal for the rock garden provided the position is not too dry and hot. All those commonly grown in gardens are perennial and quite hardy but some of the more difficult mountain species from high altitudes are better grown in pans in a frame than in the open ground, as they do not like our heavy winter rainfall and variable climate.

All gentians can be increased by seed sown in a frame or greenhouse in spring. Most kinds can also be divided carefully in spring.

Gentiana
acaulis

Geranium
sanguineum

GERANIUM *(Cranesbill)*

Here is an outstanding example of a muddle in naming, for the plant that most people commonly call geranium is not the geranium of botanists but a pelargonium. The true geraniums, are hardy herbaceous perennials or rock plants and can all be grown very easily.

One of the best for the herbaceous border is the blue geranium, *G. pratense*. It is a common wild plant in the west of England, about 2 feet in height, bearing its saucer shaped lavender-blue flowers in June and July. Even more showy in the same style is *G. grandiflorum*. *G. Endressii* has bright pink flowers and both *G. armenum* and *G. phaeum* are magenta.

For the rock garden one of the best kinds is *G. sanguineum*, another native plant often called the bloody cranesbill because of the brilliant purplish red of its flowers. A mat-forming plant, 9 inches or thereabouts in height, it blooms in June and July. An even better variety, *lancastriense*, is lower growing and has clear rose-pink flowers.

Then there are *G. subcaulescens*, a neat growing plant with small brilliantly magenta flowers on 6-inch stems in May and June, and *G. Pylzowianum*, a plant of spreading habit, reminiscent of our native herb robert, with similar bright pink flowers.

All these will grow in any ordinary soil and fairly open position and can be increased by root division in spring or autumn.

Geranium
sanguineum
lancastriense

GERBERA *(Barberton Daisy, Transvaal Daisy)*

The only species of gerbera grown in British gardens is *G. Jamesonii* a graceful and brightly coloured daisy-like flower for the greenhouse. The long, narrow petals give the flower an

Geranium
pratense

*Gerbera
Jamesonii*

*Geum
pyrenaicum*

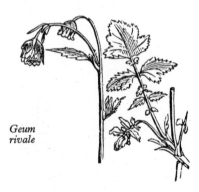

*Geum
rivale*

*Gladiolus
primulinus*

unusually elegant form, and their colours are very varied, some varieties being bright orange, others flame, salmon or pink. All are excellent for cutting as they are carried singly on slender but stiff stems about 18 inches in length.

Gerbera Jamesonii, a South African plant, is not quite hardy in this country. It needs greenhouse protection but not much artificial heat—just sufficient to keep out frost in winter. It likes a very gritty, well-drained but not poor soil and must be watered fairly freely in spring and summer, but very sparingly in autumn and winter. In fact it is not an easy plant to grow, although it can be raised fairly easily from seed. It damps off quickly if grown in soils that are too close or damp, it resents being coddled too much, yet it equally dislikes cold. Some gardeners find that it responds well to the soilless method of cultivation, i.e. grown in coarse gravel fed with a nutrient solution.

Seed should be sown in a cool greenhouse in spring and the seedlings transferred while still small either singly to small pots or about 1 foot apart in beds in which they are to flower.

GEUM *(Avens)*

There are geums for the herbaceous border and the rock garden but the former are far more popular. All the taller kinds (they average about 2 feet in height) have been derived from *Geum chiloense*, a plant with single scarlet flowers produced in succession during most of the summer. Numerous double flowered varieties have been obtained, of which the best known are Mrs Bradshaw, scarlet like its parent, Lady Stratheden, a good clear yellow, and Fire Opal, coppery red.

Geum Borisii, a smaller plant which may be grown at the front of the border or in the rock garden, is about 1 foot high and bears single bright orange-red flowers. A very good plant indeed, that is seldom without flowers from early summer to autumn.

G. rivale a rather weedy plant, $1\frac{1}{2}$ to 2 feet in height with small old-rose flowers, likes rather damp places. *G. montanum* is a better rock plant, trailing in habit, with large single yellow flowers, and *G. reptans* is similar in habit and bloom.

All are easily grown plants, not fussy about soil, but liking sunny open places. They can be increased by division in spring, or by seed sown in a frame or greenhouse in spring, but there may be some variation in colour and flower form if the double flowered varieties of *G. chiloense* are raised from seed.

GLADIOLUS *(Sword Lily)*

The gladiolus has been so highly developed by breeding that the wild species have ceased to have much importance for garden display. Three main lines may be discerned to-day, the large-flowered gladioli, for years the most popular of all; the 'primulinus' varieties which are smaller and have the hooded central upper petal derived from *Gladiolus primulinus;* and the comparatively new race of miniatures which are no larger than the primulinus varieties but have wide open instead of hooded flowers and petals which are often crimped or frilled. These miniatures are

Gloxinia
[garden form]

Helianthus
decapetalus
multiflorus

Geum coccineum
[garden form]

Hamamelis
mollis

Gypsophila
elegans

Globularia
cordifolia

Godetia
amoena
Schaminii

Helenium
autumnale
garden form]

Heliopsis
scabra

Gerbera
Jamesonii

Helianthemum
nummularium

Helichrysum
bracteatum

Gladiolus
[garden form]

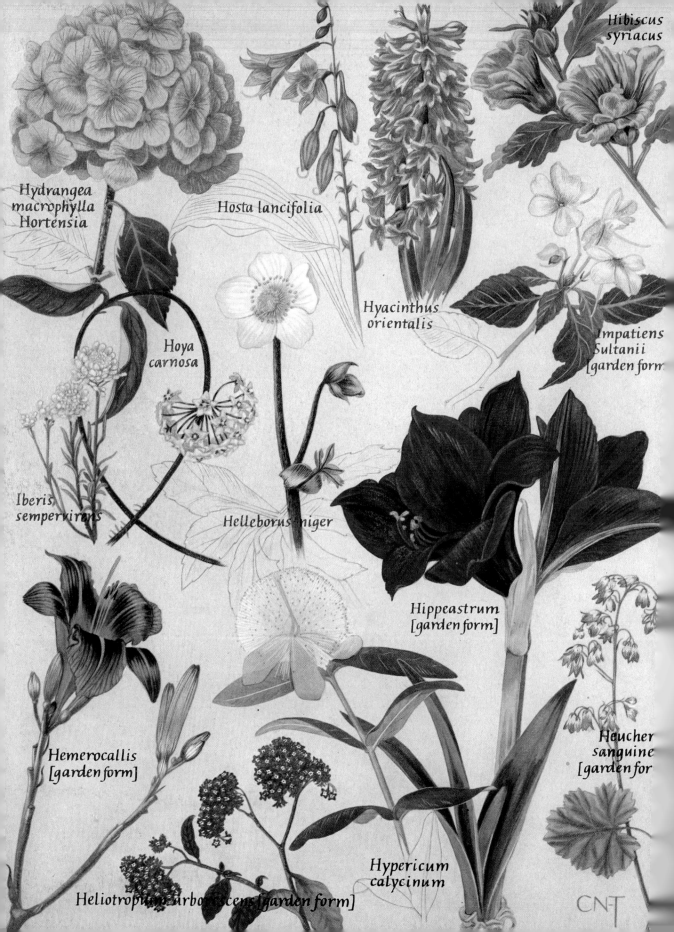

Hibiscus
syriacus

Hydrangea
macrophylla
Hortensia

Hosta lancifolia

Hyacinthus
orientalis

Impatiens
Sultanii
[garden form]

Hoya
carnosa

Iberis
sempervirens

Helleborus niger

Hippeastrum
[garden form]

Heucher
sanguine
[garden for

Hemerocallis
[garden form]

Heliotropium arborescens [garden form]

Hypericum
calycinum

CN-T

rapidly overhauling the other two classes in popularity because of their grace and their usefulness as cut flowers.

All gladioli make corms which must be protected from frost in winter. The usual practice is to plant the corms outdoors in March, April or early May, covering them with about 3 inches of soil. About six weeks after flowering, the plants are lifted and the tops cut off about an inch above the corms, which are allowed to dry for a week or so. Then the old withered corms can be detached from the bottom of the plump healthy young corms and thrown away. The new corms and also small cormlets or 'spawn' are stored in a dry, cool but frost proof place until planting time in spring.

The cormlets will not as a rule flower the first season but those of expensive varieties are worth growing on in a reserve bed until they reach flowering size in one or two years.

All gladioli like easily worked, well-drained but not dry soils. They do not need much manure but may benefit from dressings of bonemeal and hoof and horn meal before planting. They must be well supplied with moisture in summer.

In addition to these outdoor gladioli there is a race of early flowering gladioli frequently grown as pot plants in the slightly heated greenhouse. They have been derived from *G. Colvillei* and have graceful spikes of small, open, scarlet or white flowers. The corms are potted in autumn, four or five in a 6-inch pot in John Innes compost, and are grown on in a cool greenhouse, with a temperature around 50°. After flowering, watering is decreased gradually and when the foliage has died down the corms are shaken out and stored in a cool dry place until potting time.

All gladioli are readily increased by separating the young corms and cormlets when they are lifted and dried off.

Gladiolus blandus

GLOBULARIA *(Globe Daisy)*

This not very well-known family of rock plants is worth cultivation for its neat carpets of shining evergreen leaves and ageratum-like heads of fluffy mauve flowers. The two most commonly seen are *Globularia cordifolia* and *G. nudicaulis*, though *G. bellidifolia* is sometimes grown. All flower in summer, rather later than most alpines, which is an advantage. All are 4 or 5 inches in height and easy to grow in any reasonably well-drained soil and sunny position. They can be increased easily by division of the roots in spring.

Globularia cordifolia

GLOXINIA

Tuberous rooted plants for warm greenhouses, gloxinias make fine pot plants for they are neat in habit, have rich green velvety foliage and magnificent, deeply bell shaped flowers in various rich shades of purple, pink and red, often beautifully netted with one or other of these colours on a white base. Tubers can be stored dry from October to February when they are started into growth in shallow trays filled with peat or leafmould and placed in a greenhouse with a temperature of 60–65°.

Globularia nudicaulis

Gloxinia speciosa

E

*Gloxinia
digitaliflora*

*Godetia
grandiflora*

*Godetia
viminea*

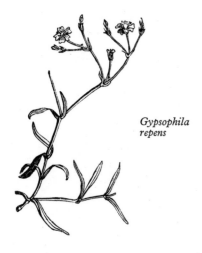

*Gypsophila
repens*

When leaves appear the tubers are potted singly in 3–inch pots in John Innes compost. Later they are moved to 5– or 6–inch pots in which they will flower. Throughout this period they must be kept in a temperature of around 65°, given plenty of moisture at the roots and around the leaves and shaded from strong sunshine. Flowers will be produced throughout the summer, and in autumn the water supply can be progressively reduced to encourage the plants to go to rest by late October.

Gloxinias can be raised from seed sown in February in a greenhouse with temperature around 65°. The seed is very small and requires careful handling and hardly any covering.

GODETIA

These are among the most useful of hardy annuals because they flower freely and are easily grown in practically any soil and sunny or partially shaded positions. The one thing you cannot do successfully with a godetia is to transplant it, so the seed must be sown direct in the open ground where the plants are to flower, in March, April, May or early September. Seedlings should be thinned to 6 to 9 inches apart according to the type being grown. Some are dwarf plants not above 8 inches in height and some are comparatively tall, reaching a height of 2 to 3 feet. Colours vary from white to crimson but some of the loveliest shades are in the pink range where the natural tendency of godetias to run to rather crude shades of carmine, has been curbed.

GYPSOPHILA

Gypsophilas may be regarded most conveniently as either perennials or annuals. The perennials are mostly derived from *Gypsophila paniculata*, which makes one very long tap root and, from that, a fine rounded bush of slender greyish stems and leaves, disappearing about midsummer or just after beneath a cloud of tiny white flowers. These are single in the wild form but there are also good double flowered varieties of which Bristol Fairy is probably the best. A variety with double lilac pink flowers is known, rather optimistically, as Flamingo.

A perennial gypsophila for the rock garden or dry wall, *G. repens* is a pretty trailing plant like a diminished and laxer version of *G. paniculata* and without its tap root. Its flowers, at their best in June, may be white or pale pink.

The annual gypsophilas are derived from *G. elegans*, a plant of loosely sprawling habit, 1 to 1½ feet high, with white flowers much larger than those of the perennials. It can be flowered from June to September by sowing seed in March, April, May and September, thinning the seedlings to 6 inches apart.

All gypsophilas like well-drained soils and *G. paniculata* is particularly happy on chalky soils. They are completely hardy but may succumb to excessive winter wet. The annuals are, of course, raised afresh each year from seed. Seed sown in a frame in spring can also be used to increase the perennials, except the fully double flowered forms of *G. paniculata* which set no seed and must be grafted in spring on to pieces of root of the single flowered variety, a tricky job, for the professional rather than the amateur. Cuttings of short young side shoots will also root in sand in July.

HAMAMELIS *(Witch Hazel)*

Hamamelis mollis is one of the best of winter flowering shrubs for it is quite hardy, easily grown, has showy and very unusual flowers and perfume. In growth it looks very like a nut bush until, in January or February, the bare branches break out into bright yellow flowers looking as if they consisted of twisted tufts of paper or wool. Their fragrance is pleasant.

There are several other species though none quite so good as *H. mollis*. *H. japonica* makes a bigger shrub and has smaller, less brilliant flowers which combine yellow and purple. It has several varieties of which *arborea* is the biggest of all. Another tree-like species is *H. virginiana* which has small yellow flowers in autumn.

They all like good loamy soils and need no regular pruning. Increase is not very easy. Rooted suckers may be detached in autumn when available, or young stems may be layered in early summer. A third possibility is to raise from seed sown in a frame in spring, but seeds may take a year and more to germinate.

HELENIUM *(Sneezeweed)*

Hardy herbaceous perennials belonging to the daisy family, extremely useful in the garden because of the solid masses of colour they give in July and August. All are very easily grown in almost any soil and reasonably open place and can be increased by division in spring or autumn.

Colours range from bright yellow to an intense chestnut red and heights vary from 3 to 6 feet. Most of the popular kinds are varieties of *Helenium autumnale*, a 6–foot plant with yellow flowers. Moerheim Beauty is 4 feet high and chestnut red, Chipperfield Orange is 6 feet and deep yellow splashed with red, Riverton Gem is similar, Mme Canivet is pale yellow with a dark centre and about 4 feet, and *pumilum* is yellow and 2 feet.

HELIANTHEMUM *(Sun Rose)*

The helianthemums are very closely allied to cistus, the rock rose, and, in fact are more often called rock roses than they are sun roses. They differ from cistuses chiefly in being on the whole far smaller and, therefore, good plants for the rock garden or dry wall. They are evergreen with thin, wiry stems and flowers which, though they fade quickly, are produced so freely and in such constant succession during May and June that they are among the most useful rock plants at that season.

Colours range from white and pale yellow through deep yellow, orange, copper, and pink to crimson. There are double-flowered as well as single forms.

All are sun lovers and like poor well-drained soils. Pruning is not essential but habit can be improved by trimming the plants

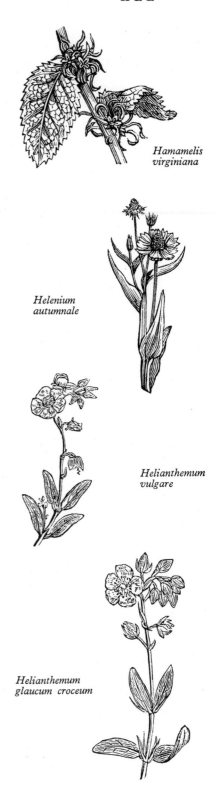

Hamamelis virginiana

Helenium autumnale

Helianthemum vulgare

Helianthemum glaucum croceum

67

Helianthus multiflorus

Helianthus rigidus

Helianthus strumosus

Helichrysum bracteatum

moderately with scissors or shears after flowering. They can be raised from seed sown in a greenhouse or frame in spring, but seedlings are likely to vary, so selected varieties must be raised from cuttings of half ripe shoots rooted in sandy soil in a frame.

HELIANTHUS *(Sunflower)*

The sunflowers give us both perennials and annuals and with few exceptions are showy plants of the easiest culture.

One fault of some of the perennials is that they are a little too vigorous and invasive. This is certainly true of that otherwise very fine plant *Helianthus rigidus*. It grows 7 or 8 feet high and carries its large yellow flowers in late summer and early August. Unfortunately it spreads by underground shoots which spring up everywhere, choking many less vigorous plants.

Helianthus sparsifolius, also known as *H. Monarch*, superficially rather like *H. rigidus*, has much finer yellow flowers each with a nearly black centre. But so far from becoming a nuisance it is often rather difficult to keep alive as it is one of the few that are not quite hardy. In many places it is necessary to lift some of the roots each autumn and place them in a frame for safety.

A really good garden plant, fully hardy and not unduly invasive, is *H. decapetalus multiflorus* a 5-foot high, August flowering plant with numerous varieties, some with double or semi-double flowers and some with single flowers of extra size.

The giant annual sunflower with huge heads of seed, so often grown for feeding poultry, is *H. annuus*. It is quite hardy and seed should be sown in March or April where the plants are to flower. As they are big seeds they can be dropped in pairs into shallow holes, 2 or 3 feet apart, the seedlings being thinned later to one at each station.

There are also smaller varieties of this species some with flowers variously marked with red, and these are better garden plants for decoration. They should be grown in exactly the same way.

The perennial sunflowers can also be raised from seed if desired, but it is easier to increase them by division.

HELICHRYSUM *(Everlasting)*

There are a number of helichrysums, only a few of which are commonly seen in gardens. The most popular is *Helichrysum bracteatum*, a hardy annual with showy double flowers made up of overlapping hard-textured petals which will retain their colour for many months. This is grown from seed sown in March or April where the plants are to flower, or alternatively, seed may be sown in frame or greenhouse in early March and the seedlings planted out 9 inches apart in May. They should be given a sunny place and a well-drained soil. The flowers are cut just before they are fully open, tied up in small bundles and suspended head downwards in a shed or similar dry but shaded place, for drying. When dry the thin stems will not support the heavy heads and wire will have to be used instead.

Ipomoea Leari

Kalanchoë
Blossfeldiana

Laburnum
vulgare

Incarvillea
Delavayi

antana
amara

Ixia
hybrida

Lamium
maculatum

apageria
rosea

Iris siberica

Kniphofia
Uvaria nobilis

Kerria japonica

Kalmia
latifolia

Jasminum
nudiflorum

CN-T

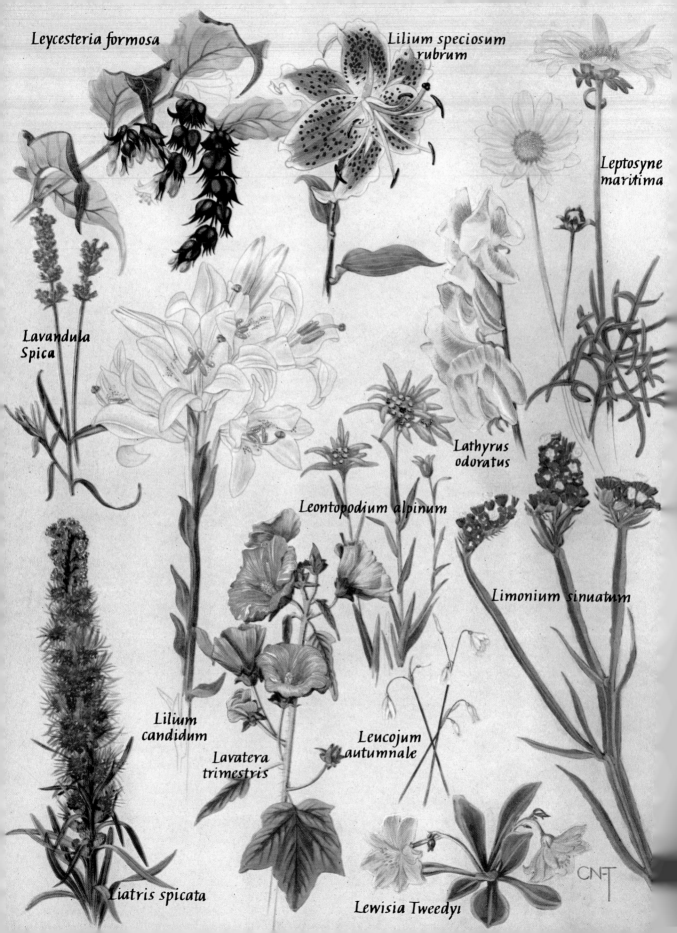

Leycesteria formosa

Lilium speciosum rubrum

Leptosyne maritima

Lavandula Spica

Lathyrus odoratus

Leontopodium alpinum

Limonium sinuatum

Lilium candidum

Lavatera trimestris

Leucojum autumnale

Liatris spicata

Lewisia Tweedyi

CNFT

An attractive plant for a rather warm, sunny place is *H. bellidioides;* a hardy or near-hardy, low-growing perennial with silvery almost globular flower heads.

H. lanatum is a good grey-leaved shrub not unlike an extremely silvery lavender in appearance and about 3 feet high. Its yellow flowers appear in July but are not particularly attractive. Treatment is as for *H. bellidioides.*

HELIOPSIS

Heliopsis helianthoides

These sunflower-like perennials for the border have the great merit that, unlike so many of the true sunflowers, they do not spread unduly but remain as compact clumps in one place. The best are *Heliopsis scabra* and its varieties *major, patula* and *zinniaeflora,* and *H. laevis.* All are about 5 feet in height and produce deep yellow flowers in August. Most have single flowers but they are double in *H. scabra zinniaeflora.*

All are completely hardy and easily grown in ordinary garden soil and open position. Increase is by division in spring or autumn.

HELIOTROPIUM *(Heliotrope, Cherry Pie)*

Heliotropium arborescens

The common heliotrope has long been a favourite summer bedding plant, both on account of its fine heads of small deep purple flowers and because of its rich perfume. Unfortunately many strains to-day seem to have little or no scent though the old fragrance is still available in certain varieties.

Heliotrope will not stand frost and should be kept in a greenhouse in winter in a temperature of around 50°; young plants can be raised from seed sown in a temperature of 60–65° in February or early March, the seedlings being pricked off and later hardened off in a frame for planting outdoors in early June. These seedlings frequently have no perfume and if scented plants are required, it is preferable to raise them from cuttings taken from plants with fragrant flowers. Cuttings may be prepared from young shoots at any time in spring or early summer, and rooted in a propagating frame with bottom heat.

HELLEBORUS *(Christmas Rose, Lenten Rose, Hellebore)*

Helleborus olympicus

None of the hellebores are showy flowers, but several of them have a quiet beauty all their own and nearly all flower in winter or earliest spring when there are few other hardy herbaceous perennials in bloom. The best known are the Christmas rose, *Helleborus niger,* with white, saucer-shaped flowers on stiff 12-inch stems in December and January, and the Lenten rose, *H. orientalis,* with dull pink to purple flowers on rather longer stems, in March and April. *H. corsicus,* a vigorous 3-foot high plant with handsome, divided leaves and great clusters of pale green flowers in January and February is well worth growing.

All these like cool, shady places and soils rich in leaf-mould or peat. They do not like disturbance and often take a year or so to settle in, especially if old clumps are moved. They can be

Helleborus niger

69

*Hemerocallis
fulva*

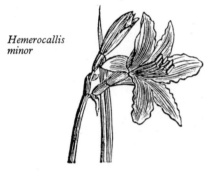

*Hemerocallis
minor*

*Heuchera
cylindrica*

*Hibiscus
Rosa-sinensis*

increased by division after flowering but in many ways it is better to start with seedlings, though seed is sometimes slow in germinating. Sow it in a frame as soon as ripe and transfer the seedlings to their flowering quarters when they have made four or five leaves.

HEMEROCALLIS *(Day Lily)*

These are lily-like flowers mostly in shades of yellow and orange though sometimes with handsome bronze or tawny markings and occasionally verging on apricot or even dull pink. The plants make fine clumps of narrow rather rush-like leaves above which the flowers are carried in clusters on slender but stiff stems 2 to 3 feet high. They open in constant succession during July and August and get their popular name of day-lilies from the fact that individually the flowers only last a day or so though there are plenty of buds to carry on the display.

They will thrive in any ordinary garden soil in either full sun or partial shade. Readily increased by division in spring or autumn, they can also be raised from seed sown in a frame in spring. The two species most commonly seen in gardens are *H. flava* with pale yellow flowers and *H. fulva* with tawny orange flowers. The latter also has a double flowered form known as Kwanso, but this is less graceful than the wild form. There are now a great many hybrids.

HEUCHERA *(Alum Root, Coral Bells)*

Graceful hardy herbaceous perennials for the front row of the border. They make low clumps of rounded leaves, often with bronzy markings, and bear in July and August loose, slender clusters of small pink or red flowers, about 2 feet in height. The most popular species, *Heuchera sanguinea*, is coral scarlet and it has produced a number of garden varieties such as Edge Hall, pink, and *splendens*, deep red. *H. brizoides gracillima* has even smaller but more numerous pink flowers and *H. tiarelloides* is not quite so tall and paler in colour. All will thrive in any ordinary soil and open or even partially shaded position. Propagation is by division in spring or autumn.

HIBISCUS *(Rose Mallow)*

From the garden standpoint the three most important hibiscus are *H. Trionum* a half-hardy annual, 18 inches high, with yellow and maroon flowers in summer, *H. syriacus*, a deciduous shrub which makes a big bush up to 12 feet in height and produces its white, blue or pink flowers in early autumn, and *H. Rosa-sinensis*, a tender shrub for the greenhouse with very showy scarlet, pink, yellow or buff flowers in summer. Seed of *H. Trionum* should be sown in a greenhouse in February or March, seedlings being hardened off for planting out in a sunny place in May or June. *H. syriacus* should be planted in a sunny rather warm place and well-drained soil. Year-old stems can be shortened a little each February. *H. Rosa-sinensis* requires a temperature of around 60° even in winter and must be given plenty of room.

70

HIPPEASTRUM *(Barbados Lily)*

These are bulbous rooted plants for the warm greenhouse. Their broadly funnel shaped flowers are carried in clusters of two to four at the top of very stout, stiff stems from March to June. They are often very brightly coloured, scarlet, crimson or pink, but there are also white forms. Most of the varieties grown are hybrids. All should be grown in a greenhouse throughout the year, but should be rested from October to February when little water will be needed and the temperature need be no more than 45–50°. After this the temperature should be increased to 60–65° and more water given. After flowering the temperature can be reduced a little and the plants placed on a shelf or staging where they get as much light as possible. A 6– or 7–inch pot will take one good bulb. John Innes compost is suitable.

Hippeastrum psittacinum

HOSTA *(Plantain Lily)*

Hostas are hardy herbaceous perennials chiefly valued for their broad leaves, bright green in some kinds such as *Hosta lancifolia*, *H. ovata* and *H. plantaginea*, grey or blue-green in others such as *H. Fortunei* and *H. Sieboldiana*, and variegated white on green in all the varieties of *H. undulata* and certain varieties of *H. Fortunei* and *H. lancifolia*. All produce loose spikes of long, more or less tubular flowers which are sometimes quite pleasing though their colours are always subdued, lilac, mauve or white. There are few better hardy foliage plants and they will thrive equally well in sun or shade, nor are they particular regarding soil though they succeed best in fairly rich soils that do not dry out too rapidly. All can be increased by division in spring or autumn. These plants are often known as funkias.

Hosta albo-marginata

HOYA *(Wax Plant)*

Hoya carnosa, the kind commonly grown, is a charming climbing plant for the slightly heated greenhouse. It is a twining plant with rather thick leaves and flat circular clusters of pale pink and white flowers that look as if they had been modelled in wax. They are produced in July and August. It is best grown in a border of fairly rich soil with plenty of peat and sand and it must have a good water supply in spring and summer, while it is growing. In winter it can be relatively dry. Thin the stems a little each February to prevent overcrowding. Temperatures should be around 45° in winter, rising to 60° or more in summer. *Hoya bella*, with white and crimson flowers, requires a considerably higher temperature.

Hoya bella

HYACINTHUS *(Hyacinth)*

The common hyacinth is a fine hardy bulb for spring bedding displays and is equally good as a house plant in bowls or as a greenhouse plant in pots or pans. Outdoors, bulbs should be planted in October or November about 8 inches apart and 4 or 5 inches deep in a well-drained, rather light but reasonably rich soil. In pots or pans for the greenhouse John Innes compost

Hyacinthus orientalis

*Hyacinthus
romanus*

*Hydrangea
macrophylla
Hortensia*

*Hydrangea
quercifolia*

*Hypericum
officinale*

may be used. The bulbs may be set almost shoulder to shoulder and should be potted in August or September. Before being brought into the greenhouse they should be placed for at least 8 weeks in an unheated frame or, better still, in a plunge bed of sharp boiler ashes, in a shady place outdoors where they can be further covered with 2 inches of ashes. Similar general treatment is also required for hyacinths in bowls except that, if the bowls have no drainage holes, soil should be replaced by bulb fibre containing peat, charcoal and crushed oyster shell. Water will be needed from the time the bulbs are potted or placed in their bowls until the foliage begins to die down the following June. They can then be allowed to dry off and the bulbs shaken out and stored in a cool dry place. Outdoor bulbs can be lifted in late June or early July and be treated in a similar manner.

HYDRANGEA

The many varieties of *Hydrangea macrophylla* are among the most showy of summer flowering shrubs. They make rounded bushes from 3 to 8 feet high and at least as much through, carrying fine heads of bloom from July to September. Colours vary according to variety and according to soil, being usually in shades of pink, red and reddish purple in soils containing much lime, and in shades of blue and blue purple in acid soils. There are also white varieties which are unaffected by soil. All will grow in sun or shade. They are reasonably hardy but severe frost sometimes injures the tips of the shoots and may prevent flowering in some varieties.

A hardier species is *H. paniculata* with fine heads of creamy white flowers in July and August. To be seen at its best it should be cut back quite a lot each March whereas the varieties of *H. macrophylla* should not be cut back though the stems can be thinned out a little each March to prevent over-flowering. *H. quercifolia*, also white flowered, has deeply scalloped leaves.

The varieties of *H. macrophylla* also make good pot plants for the slightly heated or unheated greenhouse. They can be grown in John Innes compost in large pots or tubs and must be watered freely from spring to autumn. To obtain blue flowers special blueing powder can be obtained to mix with the soil, or aluminium sulphate may be used at 1 lb. per bushel.

All hydrangeas are very readily increased by summer cuttings of young shoots inserted in a frame and watered freely.

HYPERICUM   *(St John's Wort, Rose of Sharon)*

There are herbaceous and shrubby hypericums and some of the former are quite small plants suitable for the rock garden. All are easily grown in almost any kind of soil and almost all are perfectly hardy. The best of the rock garden hypericums are *H. Coris*, *H. olympicum*, *H. fragile*, *H. repens* and *H. reptans*. None of these is above a foot in height and the last three are all trailers. All have showy yellow flowers in June and July and all like sunny places.

The true Rose of Sharon is *H. calycinum*, a low growing,

rapidly spreading evergreen shrub with brilliant yellow flowers in June and July. It will grow in sun or shade and in the poorest of soils and is a fine plant for steep banks and similar difficult places.

H. patulum is a deciduous shrub of compact habit, 3 or 4 feet high and covered in bowl shaped yellow flowers in July and August. Because of its hardiness, ease of culture and freedom of flowering, it is one of the best shrubs of medium size. There are several varieties such as *Henryi, Forrestii* and Hidcote which differ chiefly in having larger flowers.

Finest of all the shrubby hypericums in bloom is Rowallane hybrid which is 4 to 5 feet in height and produces its large golden yellow flowers in late summer. Unfortunately it is not so hardy as most and needs a sheltered position.

All hypericums can be raised from seed. The herbaceous kinds can usually be divided and the shrubby kinds increased by cuttings in summer.

IBERIS *(Candytuft)*

There are both annual and perennial candytufts. The two annuals commonly grown are *Iberis umbellata*, 1 foot high, with flattish heads of white flowers, and *I. coronaria*, a little taller, with stout, short spikes of white flowers. Both can be sown outdoors from March to May or in early September where they are to bloom and seedlings thinned to about 9 inches.

The perennial candytufts commonly seen are *I. correaefolia, I. saxatilis* and *I. sempervirens*, all bushy evergreen plants of spreading habit, not exceeding a foot in height. They have abundant white flowers in May and June and are grand plants for the rock garden or dry wall. They like sun, are not fussy about soil and can be increased by seed sown in spring or by cuttings of young shoots taken in summer and rooted in a frame.

IMPATIENS *(Touch-me-not, Balsam)*

The flowering balsam of gardens is *Impatiens Balsamina* a half-hardy annual with fine spikes of double flowers which may be pink, scarlet, violet, yellow or white. It must be raised anew each year from seed sown in a temperature of 60° from March to May. The seedlings are potted singly in small pots and are moved on to larger pots until they reach the 8- or 9-inch size in which they will flower. John Innes compost suits them well. Plenty of water should be given and frequent syringing in hot weather. The plants will flower from July to October according to time of seed sowing.

In addition there are two other fine but rather similar perennial kinds, *I. Holstii* and *I. Sultanii*. Both are soft stemmed, bushy plants about 2 feet high bearing abundant scarlet or pink flowers during most of the summer. They can be grown outdoors from June to September, but are really more satisfactory as pot plants for the greenhouse. A minimum winter temperature of 50° is sufficient and they can be raised very easily either from seed sown in a temperature of 60–65° in early spring

Hypericum
patulum

Iberis
umbellata

Iberis
coronaria

Impatiens
Roylei

73

*Incarvillea
grandiflora brevipes*

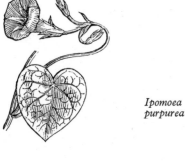

*Ipomoea
purpurea*

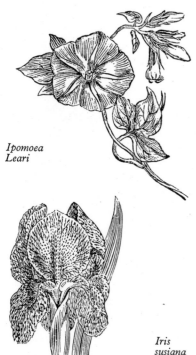

*Ipomoea
Leari*

*Iris
susiana*

or by cuttings of young shoots in a propagating box at practically any time while the plants are growing. All these balsams like plenty of water in summer.

INCARVILLEA

These are remarkable hardy herbaceous plants with showy, deeply bell shaped flowers not unlike those of the gloxinia. The flowers are usually rosy red though there is a pink kind named Bee's Pink. All flower in May and June. The species usually seen are *Incarvillea grandiflora* which is about 1 foot high, its variety *brevipes* which is a little more dwarf, and *I. Delavayi*, which is about 2 feet high. All like a sunny place and a good but well-drained soil. They have tuberous roots and can be increased either by very careful division of these roots in spring or by seed sown in a frame in spring.

IPOMOEA *(Morning Glory)*

The ipomoeas are very closely allied to convolvulus and resemble them in their widely funnel shaped flowers. They are all slender but vigorous climbers and mostly have blue flowers— sometimes an intensely pure blue as in the form of *Ipomoea rubro-caerulea* known as Heavenly Blue. *I. Leari* and *I. purpurea* (*Convolvulus major*) have flowers of a deeper hue. All flower in summer and are nearly but not quite hardy. They make good climbers for a slightly heated greenhouse (frost exclusion in winter is all that is required) or *I. caerulea* is sometimes grown as a pot plant with its slender twining stems trained around three of four bamboo canes.

All ipomoeas will grow in any reasonably good soil. They should be watered freely during spring and summer and they require no regular pruning. Propagation is by seeds sown in a warm greenhouse in spring.

IRIS

The iris family is a very large one containing plants of very different character. There are small bulbous rooted irises for the rock garden and larger bulbous rooted irises for the border. There are the very popular bearded irises flowering in May and June which like sunny places and rather dry soils, and there are irises for the bog garden. The only generalization one can make about them is that they are all perennial and nearly all hardy.

First to flower in January are small, bulbous rooted kinds such as *I. histrioides*, light blue, and *I. reticulata*, violet. They need light, well-drained soils and sheltered sunny places and their bulbs should be planted about 2 inches deep in September. The much taller bulbous rooted irises which flower in June and early July and are derived from two species *I. xiphium* and *I. xiphioides*, are divided into three sections—Spanish, English, and Dutch. Their colour range is in blue, yellow and white, and they are first-rate cut flowers. All will thrive in any ordinary soil and open place and all should be planted 3 or 4 inches deep in September.

The May and June flowering bearded irises are hybrids and they have rhizomes, i.e. fleshy root-like stems lying on the surface of the soil. There are hundreds of varieties differing chiefly in the colour of their flowers which may be anything from white and palest yellow or mauve to intense purple, deep yellow or copper. Heights vary from 2 to 5 feet. These irises may be planted in spring or autumn, or in late June immediately after flowering. The rhizomes must be kept almost on the surface when planting. They like soils well supplied with lime and sunny places but they will grow in almost any soil and position.

There are also dwarf bearded irises, often known as Crimean irises, derived from *I. Chamaeiris*. These flower in May and are suitable for the front of the border or for the rock garden.

Iris sibirica is a fibrous rooted kind with grassy foliage and it produces its rather small but very graceful blue flowers in June. It will grow in almost any soil and position but is happiest near water. It is about 3 feet high. Similar treatment is required by the tall growing yellow and white *I. ochroleuca*.

A damp soil is essential for *I. Kaempferi* a 3-foot high plant with very showy purple, violet or blue flowers in June or July. *I. laevigata*, which is rather similar in appearance, likes to grow actually in shallow water though its crowns should not be covered with more than 3 inches of water.

All the bulbous-rooted irises can be increased by dividing the clusters of bulbs. The fibrous-rooted kinds and those that produce rhizomes are increased by division.

IXIA *(African Corn Lily)*

Very beautiful and graceful bulbous-rooted plants which are on the borderline of hardiness. In mild places they can be grown outdoors but in many parts of the country they must be grown as pot plants for the cool greenhouse. All have grassy foliage and starry flowers carried on slender, 18-inch stems in June. The colour range is very wide. Bulbs should be planted or potted in October. Give them a very sunny sheltered place and well-drained soil. If potted a 4-inch pot will take about 5 bulbs. The pots should be kept in a frame for two or three months before being brought into the greenhouse. They should be watered moderately while they are making their growth and then, after flowering, the supply should be gradually cut down so that the bulbs may rest for a couple of months. Propagation is by division of bulb clusters at planting time.

JASMINUM *(Jasmine)*

The two jasmines commonly grown in gardens are *Jasminum nudiflorum* which bears its bright yellow flowers in late winter and earliest spring, and *J. officinale* which is white, fragrant and summer flowering. Both are grown as climbers but *J. nudiflorum* is a sprawling shrub rather than a true climber and will need to be tied to suitable supports. Both jasmines are very easily grown in any ordinary soil and open position. *J. nudiflorum* will even tolerate a fair amount of shade. Neither requires any

Iris pallida

Iris orientalis

Ixia viridiflora

Jasminum officinale

75

*Kalanchoë
laciniata*

*Kalmia
angustifolia*

*Kalmia
latifolia*

*Kerria
japonica*

regular pruning and both can be increased either by layering in spring or by striking cuttings of well-ripened young shoots in autumn.

KALANCHOË

These are succulents for the greenhouse and they are useful because of the ease with which most kinds can be grown and because of their brightly coloured flowers. One of the best kinds, *Kalanchoë laciniata* (or *coccinea*) produces its compact scarlet heads on 18-inch stems in summer. Others worthy of note are *K. flammea*, yellow and orange scarlet; and *K. Blossfeldiana* red. All should be grown in John Innes compost in a sunny greenhouse with minimum winter temperature of about 45°. They should be watered very sparingly in winter but moderately at other times. Re-pot when necessary in March and increase by seed sown in a warm greenhouse in spring or by cuttings placed in very sandy soil in spring or early summer.

KALMIA *(Calico Bush)*

The kalmias are evergreen flowering shrubs of great beauty but they are not the easiest of shrubs to grow as they dislike lime and require plenty of moisture, especially in summer when they are making their growth. A deep, cool, rather moist peaty soil suits them best and an open or partly shaded position.

The most popular kind is *K. latifolia* a compact bush 6 or 8 feet high bearing in June, pink flowers, curiously shaped like little Chinese lanterns. *K. angustifolia*, a much dwarfer shrub with rosy-red flowers in June, is occasionally seen and so is *K. polifolia* (*glauca*) which is not over 2 feet high and produces its rose-purple flowers in April. All can be increased by seeds sown in a frame or greenhouse in spring or by layering in early summer.

KERRIA *(Batchelor's Buttons)*

The only species grown, *Kerria japonica*, is usually seen in its double-flowered form, *flore pleno*. The flowers, which appear in April and May, are yellow pompons and it is this that has given the plant its popular name. The ordinary single-flowered form is also worth growing. The kerria makes a loose rather sprawling rapidly spreading shrub with cane-like growths. It is often treated as a climber for which purpose it must be tied up to some suitable support and pruned severely each year after flowering, the flowering stems being cut out to make way for the young shoots. It is perfectly hardy, very easily grown in sun or shade and not in the least fussy about soil.

Propagation is by layering or by summer cuttings which may need a little bottom heat to make them form roots.

KNIPHOFIA *(Red Hot Poker, Torch Lily)*

These are very handsome perennial plants for the border but unfortunately not all are thoroughly hardy. Quite reliable are *Kniphofia Uvaria* and all its many varieties, with stiff, stout

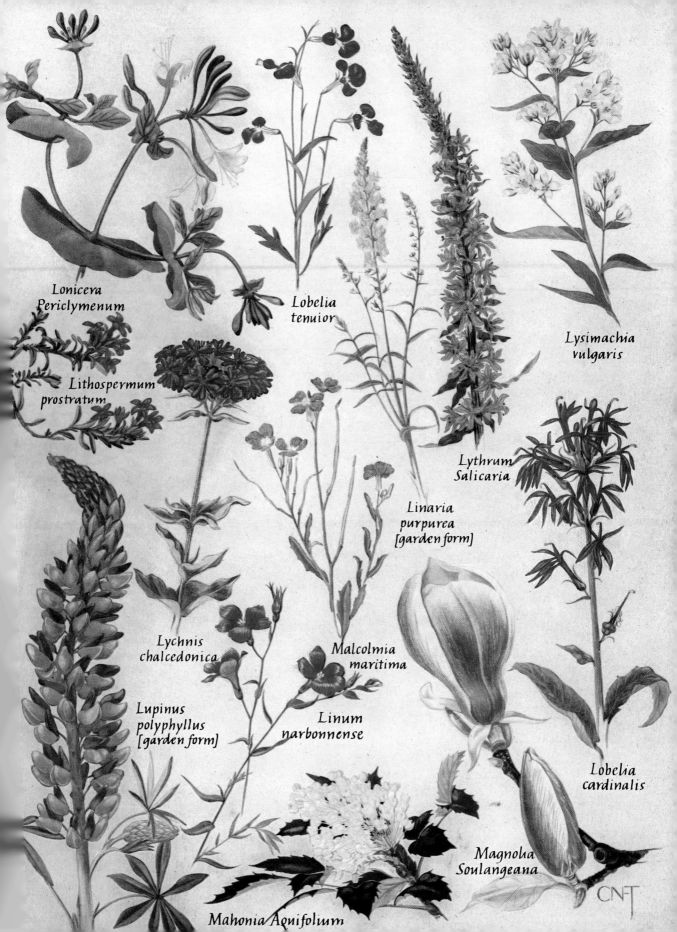

Lonicera
Periclymenum

Lobelia
tenuior

Lysimachia
vulgaris

Lithospermum
prostratum

Lythrum
Salicaria

Linaria
purpurea
[garden form]

Lychnis
chalcedonica

Malcolmia
maritima

Lupinus
polyphyllus
[garden form]

Linum
narbonnense

Lobelia
cardinalis

Magnolia
Soulangeana

Mahonia Aquifolium

CNFT

*Meconopsis
betonicifolia*

*Narcissus
incomparabilis
[garden form]*

*Narcissus
poeticus*

Montbretia
[Crocosmia
crocosmiiflora]

Malus
Lemoinei

Matthiola incana

Mesembryanthemum roseum

Mimulus
luteus

Monarda
didyma

Malope
trifida
grandiflora

Mirabilis Jalapa

Muscari
botryoides

Myosotis
dissitiflora

flower stems in July, August or September terminated by poker-shaped spikes of scarlet, yellow or scarlet and yellow flowers. Heights vary from 3 to 8 feet. Reliable also is the much smaller and more slender *K. Galpinii* with neat orange 'pokers' carried on 3-foot stems in August. A third species that seems to be quite hardy though it is seldom seen is *K. caulescens*. It has glaucous leaves and branched stems terminated by rather pale red and yellow flower spikes in June.

All these like well-drained but not dry, fairly rich soils, and full sun. They may be planted in spring or autumn but should not be frequently disturbed. They can best be increased by careful division when planting.

LABURNUM *(Golden Rain)*

The common laburnum, *L. vulgare*, is one of the most popular of spring flowering trees. Its long trails of yellow flowers are a familiar sight in May and early June. Its hybrid, *L. Vossii*, is in some respects even better as it has longer flower trails. The other parent of this hybrid, *L. alpinum*, is less familiar but a very graceful tree, a little later flowering and pleasantly fragrant.

All laburnums are easily grown in almost any soil and open position. They are not, as a rule, very long lived and sometimes die suddenly for no apparent cause, but they can be so easily raised from seed sown in spring that losses can be readily made good. No pruning is required.

LAMIUM *(Dead Nettle)*

Most of the dead nettles are weeds but one kind, *Lamium maculatum*, is a useful ground cover for rough places. It is a prostrate, trailing perennial with small, nettle shaped leaves, green with a central blotch of white. The purple flowers appear in March and April and at that season are welcome. This dead nettle will grow anywhere in sun or shade, good soil or poor and can be increased by division at any time.

LANTANA

Once popular greenhouse and summer bedding plants, these for some reason are now seldom seen. In growth they closely resemble verbenas and they have similar flat heads of flowers produced in succession during most of the summer. The colour range is yellow, red and purplish violet with many unusual intermediate shades. Their average height is 3 feet. They can be grown in pots in a frost-proof greenhouse or alternatively may be grown in a greenhouse from October to May and in a sunny place outdoors in summer. They are not fussy about soil but like sun and warmth. Propagation is either by seed sown in a slightly heated greenhouse in spring or by cuttings of young growth in spring or autumn in a frame in the greenhouse.

LAPAGERIA *(Chilean Bellflower)*

The only kind grown is *Lapageria rosea*, a very beautiful tender climbing plant with hanging, bell shaped pink flowers in sum-

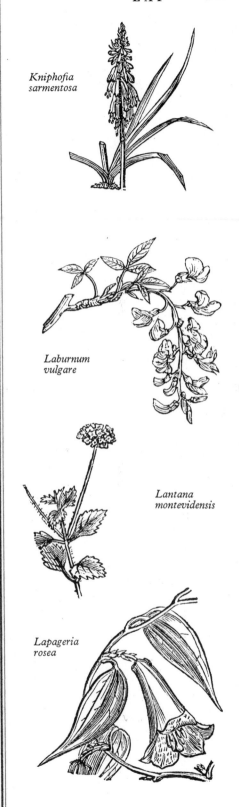

Kniphofia
sarmentosa

Laburnum
vulgare

Lantana
montevidensis

Lapageria
rosea

Lathyrus grandiflorus

Lavandula Stoechas

Lavandula Spica

Lavatera Olbia

mer. There is also a pure white form. *L. rosea* is nearly hardy and can be grown outdoors in a few very mild places, but must usually be treated as a permanent greenhouse plant. All it needs is frost protection. It is happiest when planted direct in a border of good soil and it should be well watered in summer. The slender stems should be allowed to climb on wires beneath the rafters. A little shade may be required in hot weather and frequent syringing to maintain a fairly damp atmosphere. Increase by layering in spring or early summer.

LATHYRUS *(Sweet Pea)*

Botanically the familiar sweet pea is named *Lathyrus odoratus*. It is a hardy annual which can be grown from seed sown in spring where the plants are to bloom. For the best results, however, it is preferable to sow in early September in small pots in a frame and to plant out the seedlings in well prepared rich soil the following April. There are also two systems of growing on the seedlings. One is to stick them with brushy hazel branches into which they can clamber quite naturally. By this means the largest possible number of flowers is obtained but some may be rather small. The alternative is to restrict each plant to a single stem, nipping out all side growths and tendrils, and to tie this stem to a long bamboo cane. Usually a double row of such canes is used about a foot apart and a foot from cane to cane with horizontal wires top and bottom to give additional stability. By this 'cordon' system of training the largest possible flowers are obtained, but the plants are more subject to leaf scorch.

There are a great many different varieties of sweet pea and more are added every year. It is usually wise to select up-to-date varieties as these generally give the best results.

LAVANDULA *(Lavender)*

The common lavender, *Lavandula Spica* (*officinalis*) is one of the most popular dwarf shrubs. It is grown both for its neat grey aromatic leaves which are retained all the winter and for its spikes of lavender blue, fragrant flowers in July. There are numerous varieties varying in height and in depth of colour. Hidcote variety is only a foot high and has deep purplish blue flowers. By contrast Grappenhall Variety is 4 feet high and a fairly pale lavender. There are also other species such as *L. pedunculata* with rather long stemmed flowers and *L. Stoechas* with green leaves and compact heads of purple flowers, but the common lavender is the most useful.

All lavenders like rather light, well-drained soils and sunny places. Winter wet is their enemy and on heavy, wet soils they may prove impermanent. All benefit from being trimmed over after flowering and all can be increased very easily from cuttings either in August in a propagating frame or in October outdoors.

LAVATERA *(Mallow)*

There are both annual and perennial lavateras and some are not much better than weeds but at least two are first rate garden plants. One is *Lavatera trimestris (rosea)* a hardy annual which makes a big, bushy plant 3 or 4 feet high with large, widely opened rose-pink flowers all the summer. It is rather coarse in growth but is immensely showy and as it is also very easy to grow from seed sown in March or April where the plants are to flower, it must be considered one of the ten or twelve best hardy annuals. Seedlings should be thinned to at least 18 inches.

The other outstandingly good kind is *L. Olbia*, the tree mallow, a tall shrub of loose, open habit. It will soon grow to 6 or 7 feet and produce its big, soft pink flowers all the summer. It delights in light, well-drained soils and is a first rate seaside shrub. It is not always very hardy when young and is particularly likely to suffer injury on badly drained soils. It can be quickly raised from seed sown in frame or greenhouse in spring.

LEONTOPODIUM *(Edelweiss)*

This is the alpine around which so much legend has grown up. It is by no means the difficult plant to collect or to grow that it is often supposed to be. It will thrive in any well-drained rock garden provided it is given a sunny, open position well away from the drip of trees. It is notable for its grey, silken-clad, leaves and curiously formed, rayed flowers densely clothed in white wool. It is certainly not a showy plant but it is attractive and unusual. It can be increased by dividing the roots in spring.

LEPTOSYNE

Little known but very attractive hardy annuals with yellow, daisy-like flowers. The kind most commonly seen is *L. Stillmanii* which is about 8 inches high. *L. maritima* is twice as tall. All the leptosynes are sown in April or early May where they are to flower in summer and the seedlings are thinned to 9 inches or thereabouts. They like sunny places and well-drained soils.

LEUCOJUM *(Snowflake)*

Three snowflakes are to be seen in gardens and all resemble the common snowdrop. The spring snowflake, *Leucojum vernum*, has white, green-tipped flowers on 6-inch stems in March or April. The so-called summer snowflake, *L. aestivum*, carries its nodding white, green-tipped flowers on 18-inch stems in April and May. It is followed in October by the autumn snowflake, *L. autumnale*, a smaller and more fragile plant with white, rose-tinged flowers. All like good, rather leafy, cool soils and partially shaded places and both resent disturbance. They are often slow to establish themselves and may disappoint at first. Bulbs of the spring and summer snowflakes should be planted 3 inches deep in September, those of the autumn snowflake the same depth in July or early August. Propagation is by division of the bulb clusters at planting time.

LEWISIA *(Bitterwort)*

The lewisias are extremely beautiful but not very easy rock plants. They require perfect drainage and are sometimes happiest

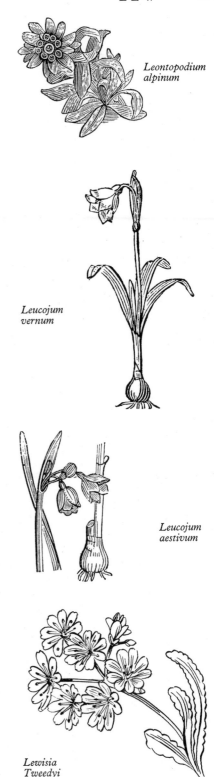

Leontopodium alpinum

Leucojum vernum

Leucojum aestivum

Lewisia Tweedyi

79

*Leycesteria
formosa*

*Liatris
spicata*

*Lilium
japonicum*

*Lilium
longiflorum*

on a dry wall where their rosettes of leaves can be disposed vertically so that they shed surplus moisture. The leaves are always rather fleshy and the flowers are carried singly or in small clusters on bare stems a few inches to a foot in length. Two of the most popular are *Lewisia Howellii* which has flowers of an unusual pinkish salmon, and *L. Tweedyi* which is not far removed from the colour of a well ripened apricot. Both flower in May and June. There are also numerous hybrids mostly with flowers in some such colours as these. All can be readily raised from seed sown in a frame in spring and as the adult plants are not likely to prove very long lived, however favourable the situation, it is desirable to keep batches of seedlings in reserve.

LEYCESTERIA *(Himalayan Honeysuckle)*

A shrub of very unusual appearance. It makes a large shuttlecock shaped clump of long, bright green, cane-like stems terminated in late summer and early autumn by short trails of chocolate and white flowers. It is hardy but the rather soft growths may be injured by frost in very cold weather. However, the plant always throws up new growths from the base and does not seem to suffer any permanent check—indeed it can, if desired, be cut back almost to ground level each February. It will grow in almost any soil and is equally happy in sun or shade. To increase it suckers can usually be detached with roots attached in either spring or autumn.

LIATRIS *(Blazing Star, Button Snakeroot)*

These curious and beautiful hardy herbaceous perennials belong to the daisy family though one might not guess that last fact from a casual glance at their close, cylindrical flower spikes. These are set with feathery looking reddish purple flowers which start to open from the top downwards. The two commonly seen are *Liatris spicata* and *L. pycnostachya* which are very similar in appearance and which both produce their 3- to 4-foot flower spikes in August. Both have small tuberous roots and both like rather moist, but not waterlogged soils. They should be planted in spring with the crowns of the tubers just below the surface. Give them a sunny place and, if the soil is inclined to dry out quickly, water them freely in summer when it is hot. All can be increased by careful division at planting time.

LILIUM *(Lily)*

This is one of the largest and most complex families of bulbous rooted plants. There are many hundreds of varieties of lily, some quite easy to grow and some distinctly difficult. Most are hardy, but a few, such as the lovely white Easter lily, *Lilium longiflorum*, are sufficiently tender to require cool greenhouse treatment.

It is difficult to generalize about lilies as their needs are so varied. Most can be planted in October or November, but a few, notably the Madonna lily, *Lilium candidum*, and the nearly allied Nankeen lily, *L. testaceum*, are better planted in late July or

Osmanthus Delavayi

Omphalodes
cappadocica

Nicotiana
Sanderae

Oxalis
adenophylla

Paeonia
officinalis rubra

Nymphaea
Marliacea

Ornithogalum
umbellatum

Nemesia
strumosa
[garden hybrids]

Nepeta
Faassenii

Olearia Haastii

Nemophila
insignis

Oenothera
fruticosa

Nerine
Bowdenii

CN-T

Petunia
hybrida

Philadelphus
Lemoinei

Papaver
orientale

Phacelia
campanularia

Passiflora
caerulea

Phlox
subulata

Phlox
paniculata
[gardenform]

Penstemon
hybrida

Phygelius
capensis

Perovskia
abrotanoides

Phlomis
fruticosa

Pernettya
mucronata

Pelargonium
zonale

CNF

early August. Most should be planted so that their bulbs are covered with about twice their own depth of soil but again there are exceptions and the Madonna lily should be just covered with soil and no more. Many lilies dislike lime and thrive best in rather acid soils but there are also many which do not mind lime and a few, such as *L. chalcedonicum*, which positively seem to like it. However, it is probably true to say there is no lily which cannot be grown in a slightly acid, lime-free soil. It is also true that all lilies like an annual top dressing of an inch or so of good leaf mould or peat and that all like to be left undisturbed for a number of years.

All lilies can be raised from seed sown in a frame or greenhouse in spring and a few, such as *L. regale* and *L. philippinense*, will flower in two or three years but most take four or five years to attain flowering size. All can be increased by careful division of the bulb clusters in autumn and many can also be increased by individual scales of bulbs carefully detached and inserted right way up in sand and peat. Some lilies, such as *L. tigrinum* and *L. Henryi*, make tiny bulbs in the axils of the leaves all up the flowering stems and these can be grown on in a few years to bulbs of flowering size.

A few of the most popular lilies are *L. auratum*, the golden-rayed lily of Japan, 6 or 7 feet tall with immense white, fragrant, gold-spotted flowers in July; *L. candidum*, the Madonna lily, 4 feet tall, with fragrant white flowers in July; *L. croceum*, 5 feet high, orange, with maroon spots, June flowering; *L. chalcedonicum*, scarlet, hanging flowers on 3-foot stems in July; *L. Henryi*, orange, purple-spotted flowers on 7-foot stems in late summer; *L. giganteum*, 10 or 12 feet high with narrowly trumpet shaped white flowers in July; *L. longiflorum*, 4 feet with white flowers in September (it is tender and can be flowered in the greenhouse at Easter time); *L. Martagon*, many shades of rose and light purple, 4 feet, June; *L. monadelphum Szovitzianum*, 3 feet, lemon yellow and July flowering; *L. pardalinum*, orange-red with maroon spots, 5 feet high and July flowering; *L. regale*, white fragrant flowers on 4-foot stems in July; *L. speciosum*, white, crimson-spotted flowers in September, 4 feet, rather tender; *L. testaceum*, light apricot, 4 feet, June-July; *L. Thunbergianum*, orange flowers carried erect on 2-foot stems in June-July; *L. tigrinum* the popular tiger lily, orange, maroon spotted flowers, on 5-foot stems in August; *L. umbellatum*, 2 to 3 feet, with yellow to orange-red flowers carried erect in June and *L. Willmottiae*, orange-red pendent flowers on 4-foot stems in July-August.

LIMONIUM *(Statice)*

These are useful plants with 'everlasting' flowers. There are both annual and perennial kinds. Best known of the annuals are *Limonium sinuatum* and *L. Bonduellii*, the first with white, blue or pink flowers, the second yellow. Both flower in July or August and are grown from seed sown in a slightly heated greenhouse in February or March, the seedlings being hardened off for planting out in a sunny position in late May or early

F

Lilium canadense

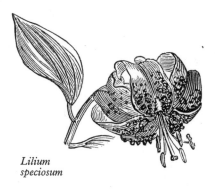

Lilium speciosum

Lilium monadelphum

Limonium sinuatum

*Linaria
purpurea*

*Linaria
bipartita*

*Linum
grandiflorum*

*Linum
flavum*

June. They should be spaced 9 inches apart in rows 18 inches apart and the flowers should be cut just before they are fully open. They are dried by being suspended head downwards for a few weeks in a cool, dry shed or room.

Best of the perennial limoniums is *L. latifolium*, which makes a large, loose spray of tiny lavender flowers in August. It grows about 2 feet high and, like the white perennial gypsophila which it slightly resembles, is an admirable flower to mix with the larger blooms. It should be planted in a sunny place and well-drained soil and be left undisturbed for as long as possible. It can be increased by root cuttings in winter.

LINARIA *(Toadflax)*

There are many different kinds of toadflax but from the garden standpoint the four most useful are *Linaria marocanna*, a hardy annual about 18 inches high, with small, snapdragon-like flowers in a variety of bright colours in summer; *L. purpurea*, a hardy perennial 3 or 4 feet high, with similarly formed, purple flowers in slender spikes from June to September; *L. pallida* (now usually known as *Cymbalaria pallida*) a small, trailing plant for rock garden or dry wall with pale purple flowers most of the summer, and *L. alpina*, a really good rock plant, tufted, 6 inches high, with purple or shrimp-pink flowers in summer.

L. marocanna is grown from seed sown in March or April where the plants are to flower. It likes a sunny position and any ordinary soil. Seedlings should be thinned to 6 inches. Less familiar, *L. bipartita*, purple and orange, requires similar treatment.

L. purpurea is very easily grown in any soil and fairly open place. It can be planted in spring or autumn and increased by division at either season.

L. pallida likes rather dry, stony places and either sun or partial shade. It is not far removed from being a weed like our own native Kenilworth Ivy, but has flowers of superior size. It can be increased by division at any time of the year.

L. alpina by contrast is worth a good place in the rock garden, in stony, quickly drained soil and a sunny place. It is best increased by seed sown in a frame in spring.

LINUM *(Flax)*

There are annual and perennial flaxes and good garden plants in each. The best annual kind is *Linum grandiflorum* which makes a slender plant about a foot high carrying wide open, scarlet flowers all the summer. It is very easily grown from seed sown in March, April or September where the plants are to flower. It loves sun and does not seem to mind how poor the soil is. Seedlings should be thinned to about 6 inches.

There are several good perennial flaxes. *L. narbonense* and *L. perenne* are very similar in appearance, about 18 inches high, narrow-leaved and carrying fine sprays of light blue flowers from June to August. *L. flavum* has bright yellow flowers and broader leaves and also flowers most of the summer. A neater and still better species with yellow flowers is *L. arboreum* which is not above a foot in height and also flowers all the summer. It is really a tiny, compact shrub.

Then there is *L. salsaloides* which brings us back to the general style of *L. perenne* but it has pearl white flowers in June and July.

All these perennial linums can be raised from seed sown in a frame in spring.

LITHOSPERMUM (*Gromwell*)

The best of the gromwells is *Lithospermum diffusum*, a low spreading plant of shrubby habit better known to gardeners as *L. prostratum*. It is notable for its intensely blue, forget-me-not flowers which are produced in greatest abundance in May and June but more sparingly for most of the summer. It is a grand plant for a sunny place on a rock garden or dry wall in lime-free soil. It has numerous garden varieties such as Heavenly Blue and Grace Ward which are distinguished by the greater size or superior colour of their flowers. All can be increased by cuttings of young shoots in a frame in July or August.

There are also other useful kinds, such as the grassy-leaved *L. graminifolium*, the loose growing *L. intermedium*, and *L. purpureo-caeruleum*, but none is quite as brilliant as *L. diffusum*.

Lithospermum purpureo-caeruleum

LOBELIA

The common blue lobelia used as an edging plant or ground cover in summer bedding schemes, needs no description, but gardeners are by no means so familiar with the erect growing scarlet and purple flowered lobelias for the herbaceous border. These are derived from three species, *Lobelia cardinalis* and *L. fulgens* both about 3 feet high with scarlet flowers, and *L. syphilitica*, similar in height but with purplish blue flowers. All flower in late summer and early autumn and like rich, cool, leafy soils well supplied with moisture. They may even be grown successfully in a bog garden or near the side of pool or stream. They are not, unfortunately, very hardy and it is wise to lift some roots each autumn and place them in a frame until the spring. They can be increased very readily by division in spring.

Lobelia Erinus

The blue bedding lobelias derived from *L. Erinus* are usually treated as half-hardy annuals, seed being sown in a slightly heated greenhouse in February or March and the seedlings hardened off for planting out in May. They should be spaced about 6 inches apart. The trailing lobelia, *L. tenuior*, is treated in the same way and is a popular plant for hanging baskets.

Lobelia fulgens

LONICERA (*Honeysuckle, Woodbine*)

This is another family that has surprises for the beginner for in addition to the well-known climbing honeysuckles with their very fragrant yellow or reddish flowers, there are a number of shrubby kinds some of which flower in mid-winter and one of which, *Lonicera nitida*, makes a fine evergreen hedge. This is grown solely for its neat, box-like foliage and it stands clipping well.

Lonicera japonica flexuosa

83

Lonicera
Brownii

Lonicera
Periclymenum

Lupinus
polyphyllus

Lychnis
chalcedonica

The two best winter flowering shrubby loniceras are *L. frag-rantissima* and *L. Standishii*. They are rather alike, both making open, 6–foot bushes bearing small cream coloured flowers which are very fragrant. Though hardy themselves their flowers may be destroyed by frost so it is desirable to give them a sheltered position. Otherwise they are not in the least difficult to grow in any ordinary soil.

There are several fine climbing honeysuckles in addition to the common British kind, *L. Periclymenum*. There are, for example, two fine varieties of this known respectively as *belgica* (or early Dutch) and *serotina* (or late Dutch). They have flowers of superior size and colour, one opening in May and June and the other in July and August.

Then there is the nearly evergreen and sweetly scented *L. japonica* and its variety *aureo-reticulata* in which the leaves are veined with gold. *L. tragophylla* has large deep yellow flowers without scent and another scentless kind worth growing for the beauty of its scarlet flowers, is *L. Brownii fuchsioides*. It is a hybrid of the beautiful but rather tender *L. sempervirens*.

All these climbing honeysuckles like rather good, loamy soils and most will grow in partial shade as well as in sun. They can be increased by layering in early summer. *Lonicera nitida* and the other shrubby kinds can be increased by cuttings of well ripened young growth in a frame in autumn.

LUPINUS *(Lupin)*

This is one of the most popular as well as one of the most improved plants for the herbaceous border. The herbaceous lupins have all been derived from *Lupinus polyphyllus*, a vigorous plant with 4-foot high spikes of pale blue or white flowers in June. Under cultivation the form and size of the spikes has been greatly improved and the colour range widened to include yellow, pink, carmine, apricot and many lovely intermediate shades or mixtures of two colours.

All are easily grown in any ordinary soil and sunny position but they do not much like very chalky soils. They can be raised quickly and cheaply from seed sown outdoors in May or in a frame in March, but seedlings usually vary a good deal in colour so selected varieties must be increased by cuttings of young shoots severed close to the crown of the plant in April and rooted in a frame. Lupins can be planted in either spring or autumn.

There is also the tree lupin, *L. arboreus*, a big bushy plant with much smaller spikes of yellow or white flowers in June and July. It is a grand seaside plant and revels in sandy soils but is usually short lived on heavier and richer soils inland. This also is easily raised from seeds or cuttings.

LYCHNIS *(Maltese Cross, Jerusalem Cross, Rose Campion)*

The three best species of lychnis for the garden are *Lychnis chalcedonica*, the Maltese or Jerusalem cross, a 3-foot high hardy perennial with brilliant scarlet heads of cross shaped flowers in July and August; *L. Coronaria*, the rose campion, a grey-leaved plant with magenta flowers in June and July, to be seen in most old cottage gardens, and *L. Viscaria splendens plena* sometimes known as the German catchfly, a smaller plant, not above a foot in height, with short spikes of light carmine, double flowers in June and July. All are sun lovers and all like rather open, well-drained soils. *L. Viscaria splendens plena* may even be grown in a dry wall though it is really a front row plant for the border. All can be increased by careful division in spring.

LYSIMACHIA *(Loosestrife)*

The yellow loosestrife, *Lysimachia vulgaris*, is a very easily grown hardy perennial for shady places and damp soils. It produces 3-foot spikes of yellow flowers in June and July and can be increased by division in spring or autumn. There are other kinds worth growing though none is better than *L. vulgaris*. *L. punctata*, also known as *L. verticillata*, is rather more graceful in habit and *L. clethroides* has white flowers but is not so indestructible.

LYTHRUM *(Purple Loosestrife)*

The two kinds of lythrum commonly grown in gardens have slender spikes of magenta flowers in July and August. They thrive well in damp places but may also be grown quite successfully in the border in ordinary soil and with good drainage. The two species are *L. Salicaria* and *L. virgatum* and they differ chiefly in the fact that the flower spikes of *L. Salicaria* are rather stouter and the individual flowers are larger than those of *L. virgatum*. There are several forms of *L. Salicaria*, two of which, Rose Queen and Lady Sackville, have flowers of a pure rose-pink colour. All can be increased by division in spring or autumn.

MAGNOLIA *(Cucumber Tree, Yulan, Lily Tree)*

Most of the popular magnolias are either large shrubs or small trees and they are grown for the beauty of their flowers. These are carried erect in most of the spring flowering kinds such as *M. denudata*, *M. Soulangeana*, *M. Kobus*, *M. salicifolia* and *M. stellata* and are not unlike a tulip in shape for which reason they are often referred to as tulip trees though this name properly belongs to *Liriodendron tulipifera*. In contrast there is a summer flowering group of magnolias, including *M. sinensis*, *M. Watsonii*, *M. highdownensis* and *M. Sieboldii* in which the flowers are saucer shaped and hang downwards. They are white with a central boss of crimson and are both beautiful and fragrant. The spring flowering kinds are not, as a rule, so powerfully scented (some are not scented at all) and their flowers are white, pink or purple. All these are deciduous. In addition there are two notable evergreen kinds, *M. grandiflora* which has large shining green leaves not unlike those of a laurel, and fine white flowers shaped like water lilies, and *M. Delavayi* with darker, less shining leaves and

Lychnis Viscaria

Lythrum virgatum

Magnolia grandiflora

Magnolia denudata

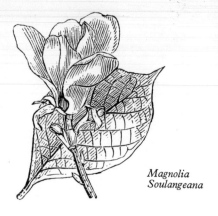

Magnolia
Soulangeana

Mahonia
Aquifolium

Malcolmia
maritima

Malope
malacoides

white flowers which are not so freely produced.

Magnolias prefer slightly acid soils though many of them will grow on neutral or even slightly alkaline soils. They do not like being disturbed and are not always easy to transplant but the best time to move them is in spring or early autumn. They are hardy enough but as some flower so early it is advisable to give them a sheltered position as protection for their bloom.

The usual methods of propagation are by layering the young stems in late spring or early summer or by grafting on to nearly allied species which may themselves be raised from seed.

MAHONIA

These evergreen shrubs are closely allied to the barberries. They are easily grown but not all are completely hardy. One of the best, *Mahonia Aquifolium*, has holly-like leaves, makes a compact shrub 3 or 4 feet high and produces its clusters of small, clear yellow flowers from February to May. It is fully hardy. *M. japonica* and the very similar *M. Bealei* flower in winter and their yellow flowers are borne in a circle of radiating spikes like the spokes of a wheel. They are extremely handsome shrubs and are fairly hardy but need a sheltered place because of their winter flowering. *M. lomariifolia* makes great rosettes of long, pinnate leaves and is a very handsome foliage plant quite apart from the beauty of its yellow flowers, but it is rather apt to get bare at the base and acquire a gaunt, ungainly habit and it is not very hardy.

Mahonias will grow in most ordinary soils, none needs any regular pruning and all can be increased by autumn cuttings. *M. Aquifolium* can also be increased by division in spring or autumn.

MALCOLMIA   *(Virginian Stock)*

The Virginian stock, *Malcolmia maritima*, is a pretty little annual, quite hardy and so easily raised from seed sown where it is to flower, that it can be grown practically anywhere. It is 6 inches or so in height, has confetti-like flowers in various shades of pink, lilac and white, and, if sown successively from March to May with a final sowing in September, will give a supply of flowers most of the summer. It is particularly useful as an edging plant, for filling bare places in the rock garden or for crevices between paving slabs.

MALOPE

The usual species of malope grown in gardens, *M. trifida*, is a hardy annual which makes a big, bushy plant not unlike a lavatera in habit and flower, but rather more crude in colour. The widely open, funnel shaped flowers are a rather fierce magenta, effective in the right place but not always easy to associate. This is a very easily grown plant not in the least fussy about soil but preferring sunny places. Seed should be sown in March, April and September where the plants are to flower and the seedlings should be thinned to about 18 inches apart.

86

MALUS *(Apple)*

There are numerous kinds of crab apple as well as other nearly allied species of malus which are useful ornamental trees or large shrubs. One of the best of these, *M. floribunda*, a small tree, bears small but abundant flowers in April and early May. They are red in bud but pale pink when fully open. *M. Lemoinei* makes a rather larger tree, perhaps 25 feet high when full grown, and it has bigger, deep carmine flowers and purple foliage. Very similar in appearance are *M. aldenhamensis* and *M. Eleyi* and all three usually carry good crops of purple, cherry-like fruits. Then there are the true crab apples such as Dartmouth, with round purplish red fruits and John Downie with oval yellow and red fruits. The Siberian crab has smaller, round fruits very freely produced, yellow in one variety and red in another.

They will grow in any ordinary garden soils and open positions. They need not be regularly pruned but can be thinned out and cut back a little in autumn if they become overgrown. All can be raised from seed sown outdoors in March but there is usually some variation in the seedlings, for which reason selected varieties are usually grafted in spring or budded in summer.

MATTHIOLA *(Stock)*

There are several very distinct types of stock grown in gardens but they have all been derived from one native seaside plant, *Matthiola incana*. The principal garden kinds are the ten-week stocks which are grown as half-hardy annuals, East Lothian stocks which may be treated as half-hardy annuals or as hardy biennials and Brompton stocks which are always grown as hardy biennials. All make bushy plants with fine spikes of fragrant flowers which may be single or double though the doubles are always more highly prized. The colour range is from white and palest mauve or pink to pale yellow, deep purple and crimson.

Seed of the ten-week stocks is sown in a greenhouse or frame, in a temperature of 55° in March, seedlings being pricked off and then hardened off for planting out in late May or early June. Alternatively seed can be sown in late June to give seedlings to flower in a warm greenhouse in winter.

The East Lothian stocks can either be sown in February and treated like ten-week stocks when they will flower in late summer, or they can be sown in August, the seedlings overwintering in a frame and planted out in April to flower in July.

Brompton stocks are sown outdoors towards the end of June, the seedlings being transferred to a nursery bed of good soil in an open place as soon as they can be handled conveniently, and finally removed to their flowering quarters in October or March. In cold districts they are best overwintered in a frame.

MECONOPSIS *(Himalayan Poppy, Blue Poppy, Welsh Poppy)*

The most famous species of meconopsis is undoubtedly *M. betonicifolia*, the Himalayan blue poppy, a beautiful hardy peren-

Malus
pumila

Malus
floribunda

Matthiola
incana

Meconopsis
cambrica

*Meconopsis
napaulensis*

*Mesembryanthemum
crystallinum*

*Mesembryanthemum
acinaciforme*

*Mimulus
luteus*

nial 3 to 5 feet high bearing large, saucer shaped sky blue flowers in July and August. It is not the easiest of plants to grow as it is fussy about soil and position, liking best a deep cool, leafy or peaty soil and a partially shaded place. It can be raised from seed sown in sandy peat in a frame in spring but seedlings often vary considerably and many may give flowers of an inferior amethyst.

There are many other species mostly with similar requirements and many of them not long lived. Typical of the family is *M. integrifolia*, the Chinese yellow poppy, 3 feet high with large pale yellow flowers. It always dies after flowering and so must be frequently renewed from seed. *M. napaulensis* (*Wallichii*) has pale blue flowers and very handsome foliage covered with tawny hairs. *M. cambrica*, the Welsh Poppy, is rather like a miniature Iceland poppy with pale yellow flowers and in half shady places it often takes complete control, reproducing itself so rapidly from self-sown seed that it ousts everything else.

MESEMBRYANTHEMUM *(Ice Plant)*

These half-hardy succulent plants, mostly of trailing habit, have highly coloured flowers which have a superficial resemblance to those of the daisy family though they are, in fact, quite unrelated. There are a great many kinds and naming is rather confused. Among the best for garden purposes are *Mesembryanthemum aurantiacum*, more erect than most and with fine orange flowers; *M. Brownii*, not unlike the last but smaller in all its parts and, if anything, even brighter in colour; *M. criniflorum*, prostrate, red, pink or white and one of the few annuals in the family; *M. roseum*, trailing and with rose pink flowers, and *M. crystallinum*, the true ice plant, so-called for the glistening, translucent pustules which cover it. It is a trailing annual with whitish or very pale pink flowers. In seaside districts the vigorous *M. acinaciforme* often grows wild.

All love sun; it seems to be impossible to find a place too hot and dry for them and they delight to scramble over stones or to cascade down sunny walls. The perennials can be increased by cuttings of young shoots in summer or early autumn and the annuals by seed sown in a warm greenhouse in spring. As they are all likely to be killed by a few degrees of frost, it is wise to keep some stock in a frost-proof greenhouse or frame in winter.

MIMULUS *(Monkey Flower, Musk)*

There are both annual and perennial species of mimulus, several of which are gay plants for garden or greenhouse. The perennials are mostly moisture lovers which can be grown in damp parts of the rock garden, at the side of pools or streams or even in the bog garden. Examples of this kind are *Mimulus luteus* and *M. guttatus*, two very similar plants, 12 to 18 inches high with yellow, red-spotted flowers in summer, and *M. cupreus*, half as high and copper coloured. There are many garden varieties of these, one of the finest of which is the dwarf and very brilliant Whitecroft Scarlet.

The annual kinds are usually hybrids and they are often described as *M. tigrinus*, a name of doubtful validity. They produce large, pouched flowers in various shades of yellow and crimson usually heavily spotted or blotched with one colour on the other. Seed should be sown in a slightly heated greenhouse or frame in February or March and the seedlings pricked out and hardened off for planting out in late May. They like fairly rich and well-watered soil.

*Mimulus
moschatus*

The old-fashioned musk, famous for the fact that it has mysteriously lost its scent, is little grown nowadays. It is *M. moschatus*, a plant for the cool greenhouse in which it can be grown either from seed sown in March or from cuttings of young growth in spring or summer.

MIRABILIS *(Marvel of Peru, Four O'clock Plant)*

The only kind of mirabilis likely to be seen in English gardens is *Mirabilis Jalapa*. It has been called the four o'clock plant because its fragrant yellow, red, white or variously blotched flowers tend to open in the afternoon and keep closed when the sun is shining brightly. It is a perennial, very readily raised from seeds sown in a warm greenhouse in spring and quickly making large, tuberous roots which plunge deeply into the soil. It can be grown outdoors in summer in warm, sunny positions but is killed by frost so must either be renewed annually or be over-wintered in a greenhouse. It grows about 3 feet high, makes a fairly big, leafy plant and flowers profusely from midsummer until the autumn.

*Mirabilis
Jalapa*

*Monarda
Russelliana*

MONARDA *(Bergamot, Bee Balm)*

Hardy herbaceous perennials related to the sages and with a pleasant aromatic perfume. The only species commonly grown is *Monarda didyma* but this has numerous garden varieties differing in colour. All are bushy plants 2 to 3 feet high. The common form has scarlet flowers but there are varieties with white, mauve, violet, purple and pink flowers. All are very easily grown in any ordinary soil and fairly open position, and all can be increased by division in either spring or autumn.

MONTBRETIA

The familiar garden plant which everyone knows as a montbretia will be found in modern botanical works of reference as *Crocosmia crocosmiiflora*. It is a hardy plant producing innumerable small corms by separating which it can be easily and rapidly increased. It loves warm, sunny places and does not seem to mind how poor the soil is so long as it is fairly well drained. The orange coloured flowers are borne on slender spikes in August and September. There are many improved varieties with flowers of greater size and extending the colour range from clear yellow to crimson, but few of these are either as hardy or as easy to grow as the common type. Some must even be lifted each autumn and overwintered in a frame to be planted out the following April and most of these improved forms prefer fairly rich, well-worked soils such as would be prepared for gladioli.

*Montbretia
(Crocosmia aurea)*

*Muscari
racemosum*

*Myosotis
sylvatica*

*Narcissus
triandrus*

*Narcissus
Bulbocodium*

MUSCARI *(Grape Hyacinth)*

Small early flowering, bulbous-rooted perennials that are ideal for the front of a border or for massing in the rock garden or beneath shrubs. The most popular kind is *M. botryoides* which has 6-inch high spikes of clear blue flowers. It has numerous varieties including a white and one named Heavenly Blue which is a deeper and purer blue. There is also an interesting kind known as the feather hyacinth, *M. comosum monstrosum*. This has much larger flower spikes, which may be 12 inches long but arch or flop more or less horizontally. The blue flowers have a feathery appearance and are most attractive.

Bulbs of these and other grape hyacinths should be planted in autumn, 2 to 3 inches deep in ordinary soil and a sunny position. They can be increased by dividing the bulb clusters at planting time. It is not desirable to lift the bulbs annually.

MYOSOTIS *(Forget-me-not)*

All the familiar kinds of forget-me-not are hardy perennials but the common kinds used for spring bedding and derived from several species, including *Myosotis caespitosa*, *M. dissitiflora* and *M. sylvatica*, are not easy to keep after flowering and are so readily raised from seed that they are nearly always treated as biennials. Seed is sown outdoors in June or early July, the seedlings are pricked out in a nursery bed and are transferred to their flowering quarters in October. They will grow in practically any soil or place and do not object to some shade. In wild parts of the garden they will often naturalize themselves, coming up year after year from self-sown seed without any attention.

There are also choicer and more compact kinds of forget-me-not for the rock garden, such as *M. alpestris*, and for the edge of the water garden or the bog there is the true forget-me-not, *M. palustris* *(scorpioides)*. This is a rather looser plant with pale blue flowers each with a yellow eye.

NARCISSUS *(Daffodil)*

One of the most popular families of hardy bulbous rooted plants and one which has been so highly developed in gardens that varieties run into thousands. To avoid confusion these have been arbitrarily divided into a number of sections distinguished by the form and general colour of the flowers. Those with long central crowns are known as trumpet daffodils and those with short crowns as small-cupped narcissi. Then there are double-flowered varieties and varieties which bear numerous small flowers on one stem. The poet or pheasant-eye narcissi all have very small flat cups, the colour of which is ringed in the manner of *Narcissus poeticus*. The jonquils have small very fragrant flowers in clusters.

In addition there are the numerous wild species some of which are extremely beautiful and distinctive. There is, for example, the cyclamen-flowered daffodil, *N. cyclamineus*, only a few inches in height and with tubular crowns and narrow, reflexed perianth segments. It is an exquisitely dainty flower. So is the hoop-petticoat daffodil, *N. Bulbocodium*, another miniature with the crown shaped like a tiny crinoline and the surrounding segments very narrow. The angel's-tears daffodil, *N. triandrus*, is 6 to 9 inches in height and has clusters of small, nodding white flowers and *N. Tazetta* is also multiflowered.

All these thrive in good loamy soils and should be planted in August, September or October. Cover their bulbs to about twice their own depth. They can be naturalized in grass but the grass must not be cut until the daffodil foliage has died down in late June or early July.

Propagation is by division of the bulb clusters in July but it is not desirable to lift daffodils annually. They are best left undisturbed until they become overcrowded.

Narcissus
Tazetta

NEMESIA

There are few more beautiful annuals than *Nemesia strumosa* and its many garden varieties, but it is a plant that needs a little more care than many annuals. The thing to avoid above all others is to get the seedlings starved and prematurely in flower before they are planted out. For this reason it is wise not to start too early. Seed can be sown in a greenhouse or frame in late March or early April and the seedlings pricked off into good soil as soon as they can be handled. They should then be hardened off carefully for planting out in late May or early June. Give them a sunny position and rather rich soil and space them 6 to 9 inches apart. The average height of the plants is about 12 inches but there are dwarf forms not exceeding 6 inches. The colour range includes yellow, orange, red, blue and white.

Nemesia
floribunda

NEMOPHILA *(Baby Blue-eyes)*

Nemophila insignis is a pretty blue-flowered hardy annual which deserves to be better known than it is. It only grows about 6 inches high and may be had in flower most of the summer if three or four sowings are made between mid-March and mid-May. Sow the seed where the plants are to flower, preferably in a sunny place but in any ordinary soil, and thin the seedlings to 4 inches apart. *N. maculata* has white purple-spotted flowers.

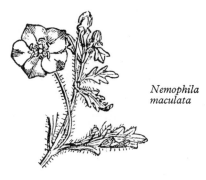

Nemophila
maculata

NEPETA *(Catmint)*

The catmints are hardy perennials mostly with rather aromatic leaves. The best known is the plant always listed, though incorrectly, as *Nepeta Mussinii* (its real name is *N. Faassenii*). It is a bushy plant usually about 15 inches high, though there are taller forms, with greyish leaves and slender spikes of small lavender blue flowers. The effect is very attractive and the plant goes on flowering almost all the summer. It likes well-drained places and does not seem to mind how poor the soil is. It makes an excellent edging to a border and is also very happy in a dry wall. It is quite hardy but tends to die in winter on cold, wet soils. It is very easily propagated by division in the spring.

A very different kind is *N. hederacea* (*Glechoma*) a slender

Nepeta
hederacea

91

Nerine
sarniensis

Nicotiana
Tabacum

Nymphaea
caerulea

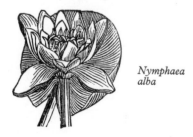

Nymphaea
alba

trailing plant with light blue flowers. It has a variety with silver variegated leaves which is sometimes grown in hanging baskets and window boxes. It is quite hardy, not in the least fussy and easily increased by division.

NERINE *(Guernsey Lily)*

The name Guernsey lily is really applied to one nerine only, *Nerine sarniensis*, which has roundish heads of scarlet flowers carried in early autumn on leafless stems 18 inches tall. The leaves appear as the flowers fade. This kind is too tender to be grown outdoors and needs the shelter of a frost-proof greenhouse which is also true of the kind commonly known as *N. Fothergillii*, which is very similar in general appearance, and of the many hybrids which are sold under fancy names and which have flowers in various shades of red and pink. By contrast the rose pink flowered *N. Bowdenii* can be grown outdoors in very sunny, sheltered places, as at the foot of a wall facing south. It is not quite so tall and flowers in late summer.

All these nerines have bulbous roots. The greenhouse varieties should be potted in July or August, in John Innes compost, one bulb in a 4-inch pot or three bulbs in a 6-inch pot. Water moderately during the flowering and growing period, roughly from late August to May, but keep almost dry in June and July. They like full sun at all times.

Bulbs of *N. Bowdenii* should be planted in July, being covered with about 3 inches of soil.

NICOTIANA *(Tobacco)*

The true tobacco is *Nicotiana Tabacum*, a large, rather weedy annual which is grown solely for its leaves. There are, however, numerous ornamental kinds of nicotiana of which the best are *N. alata grandiflora* (*affinis*) often known as the sweet scented tobacco or the jasmine tobacco, and *N. Sanderae* the red flowered tobacco. These are both grown as half hardy annuals, seed being sown in a warm greenhouse in February or March and the seedlings pricked out and hardened off for planting outdoors in late May or early June. Both make plants 3 or 4 feet high with showy flowers which are white in *N. alata*, carmine in *N. Sanderae*. They are not particular about soil and will thrive in full sun or partial shade. The fragrance is most marked at night.

NYMPHAEA *(Water Lily)*

The hardy water lilies are all species of nymphaea and there are also some kinds, such as *N. caerulea*, the blue lotus of Egypt and *N. stellata*, the blue lotus of India, that are tender aquatics which must be grown in a warm greenhouse. All must have their roots in water all the year but there are individual preferences as to the depth of the water. For example *N. alba*, the common white water lily, and *N. Gladstoniana*, another kind with large white flowers, both like fairly deep water, say 2 feet or even 3 feet. By contrast *N. tetragona*, the pygmy water lily, with small white flowers, and its pale yellow variety *helvola*, both thrive best in water no more than 4 or 5 inches deep. The majority of the popular hybrids, known under the general name *N. Marliacea*, will grow well in water 1 to 2 feet deep.

Most make fleshy or tuberous roots and should be planted just as growth is starting in April or May. They can be planted in ordinary soil in the bottom of a pool or may be planted in boxes, baskets or wire cages filled with good rich soil and then sunk in position. Propagation is by division at planting time.

OENOTHERA   (*Evening Primrose*)

The common evening primrose, *Oenothera biennis*, is a tall, rather weedy biennial with very beautiful pale yellow flowers of fragile build which open in the evening. It is a good plant for rough places and one that will thrive in very poor soils and sunny or partially shaded positions. It flowers in July and August. It is easily grown from seed sown in May or June where the plants are to bloom the following year.

A better garden plant is *O. fruticosa*, a bushy perennial 18 to 24 inches high, delighting in rather light, well-drained soils and producing a profusion of bright yellow flowers in July and August. It has several varieties such as *Youngii* and *major*, differing mainly in being rather more compact in habit or even more showy in flower. All are good perennials in well-drained soils and all can be increased by division in spring.

There are also dwarf oenotheras for the rock garden, notably *O. missouriensis*, a low-growing, grey-leaved plant with fine light yellow flowers in late summer; *O. mexicana* with soft pink flowers, and *O. acaulis* (*taraxacifolia*) with white or pink tinted flowers. All want the best possible drainage and full sun.

OLEARIA   (*Daisy Bush*)

There are many kinds of olearia but unfortunately most of them are a little too tender to be fully reliable outdoors except in the mildest parts of the country. All are evergreen shrubs with daisy-like flowers. One of the best for general planting is *Olearia Haastii*, a big bush of dense, rounded habit with neat oval leaves and masses of small white daisy flowers in July and August. Hardy enough for most places, it is not in the least fussy about soil and usually does well in towns.

Another good kind, *O. stellulata* (*Gunniana*), is about 5 feet high, has small grey leaves and white flowers. It is not as hardy as *O. Haastii* but does well in many parts of the country.

Very different in appearance is *O. macrodonta*, which may grow to a height of 20 feet but can be kept much smaller by a little judicious pruning each spring, and has large holly-like leaves and white flowers. In some mild places it is grown as a hedge.

All can be increased by cuttings of firm young shoots in July or August in a propagating frame.

OMPHALODES   (*Navel-wort*)

These are small and very pretty perennial plants with blue flowers rather like forget-me-nots. One of the best is *Omphalodes*

Nymphaea micrantha

Oenothera Drummondii

Oenothera biennis

Olearia stellulata

*Omphalodes
verna*

*Ornithogalum
narbonense*

*Osmanthus
fragrans*

*Oxalis
rosea*

Luciliae, a neat tufted plant about 6 inches high which flowers in May. *O. verna* is coarser in growth and sprawling in habit, 8 or 9 inches high with abundant blue flowers in April and May. It is sometimes called the creeping forget-me-not. *O. cappadocica* has blue-grey leaves and the usual blue flowers.

Both *O. verna* and *O. cappadocica* will grow in shade or sun and almost any kind of soil. *O. Luciliae* needs sun and reasonably well-drained soil. It is really a plant for the rock garden. All can be increased by division in the spring.

ORNITHOGALUM *(Star of Bethlehem)*

The true star of Bethlehem is *Ornithogalum umbellatum*, a hardy bulbous-rooted plant with loose, foot high sprays of starry white flowers in June. Not unlike it but with narrower spikes and nodding flowers is *O. nutans* which flowers at the same time. Both are useful plants for odd corners and difficult places for they will thrive in almost any soil and do not mind full sun or partial shade. Both can be increased by division in the autumn.

OSMANTHUS *(Fragrant Olive)*

Without doubt the best osmanthus for general garden planting is *Osmanthus Delavayi*, a first-class evergreen shrub, freely branched and dense in habit, with small, very dark green leaves and tiny white tubular flowers produced with great freedom in April. They are notable for their extremely sweet fragrance which is often air-borne for many yards around a plant. Another occasionally grown, principally for its dark green holly-like leaves, is *O. Aquifolium*. Both like good, loamy soils and though both may be considered hardy in most parts of the country, *O. Delavayi* should be given a little protection until it is firmly established and growing well. Neither requires any regular pruning and both can be increased by cuttings of firm young shoots in a propagating frame in July or August. *O. fragrans*, up to 30 feet high, requires greenhouse protection.

OXALIS *(Wood Sorrel)*

The British wood-sorrel, *Oxalis Acetosella*, is a pretty carpeting plant with clover-like leaves and fragile pearl white flowers in spring, but it spreads so rapidly that it must be considered a bad weed in gardens. Not so *O. adenophylla* and *O. enneaphylla*, two lovely rock plants which never spread far or make themselves a nuisance. Both have tuberous roots and grey leaves but the fine flowers are white veined with lilac pink in *O. adenophylla* and white in *O. enneaphylla*. Neither exceeds 3 inches in height and both revel in sun and rather light, well-drained soils. Another very popular kind is *O. rosea* (or *rubra*) a prostrate plant with clover-like leaves and loose sprays of light rose flowers most of the summer. It loves sun and warm dry places and may often be seen in old cottage gardens tucked in under a sunny wall or growing in the crevices of a path. It also makes a useful pot plant for a sunny window.

O. rosea can be easily increased by division at practically any time of the year. *O. enneaphylla* can also be divided in spring but *O. adenophylla* must be raised from seed sown in a greenhouse or frame in spring.

PAEONIA *(Peony)*

Three types of peony are commonly grown in British gardens, the common peony derived from *Paeonia officinalis*, the Chinese peonies derived from *P. albiflora*, and the tree peonies derived from *P. suffruticosa (Moutan)*. The first and second are hardy herbaceous perennials, usually about 3 feet high with single or, more commonly, large double flowers in June. They differ in that though the colour range in both is from white, through pink to crimson, there is a greater variety of shades in the Chinese than in the common peony and they are fragrant. Many of the loveliest flowers are to be found in the Chinese type.

Varieties of *P. suffruticosa* are all rather soft-stemmed shrubs and they are not quite so easy to grow as the other two groups. Plants average 6 feet in height and they produce their very large, usually fully double flowers in June. The colours are varied and often very beautiful, covering white, pink, crimson, apricot and many intermediate shades or combinations of two or more colours.

They like good, rich, loamy soils not inclined to dry out too severely, and thrive in sun but will succeed in light shade. They dislike being moved and usually take a year or so to recover and start flowering freely again.

All can be planted in spring or autumn. The herbaceous kinds are usually increased by division, the tree peonies by grafting, often on to herbaceous peony roots though this is not really a practice to be commended.

PAPAVER *(Poppy)*

The poppies are a gay lot and all are easy to grow. There are both annual and perennial kinds, the two most important in the first class being the Shirley poppies and the opium poppies, and the two best in the second group, the oriental poppies and the Iceland poppies.

The Shirley poppies are derived from our own native field poppy, *Papaver Rhoeas*, but instead of being all scarlet like that brilliant but troublesome plant, they have flowers of every shade from white and palest pink to scarlet, some combining two shades, some single flowered and some double and all beautiful.

The opium poppies are derived from *P. somniferum*, a rather more robust plant with smooth greyish green leaves. Most modern strains have large double flowers and the colour range is from white to purple.

Both these annual poppies are grown from seed sown in March, April, May or September where the plants are to flower. The seedlings should be thinned to 9 inches, or thereabouts. They like a sunny place and do not mind how poor or dry the soil is.

95

Paeonia suffruticosa

Paeonia albiflora

Papaver Rhoeas

Papaver somniferum

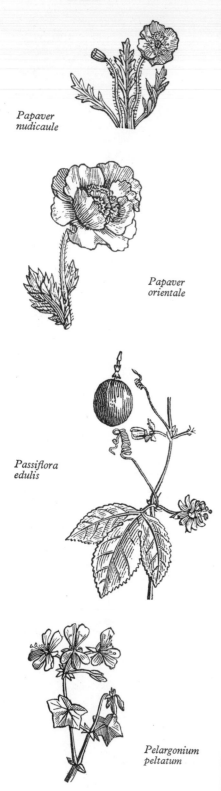

*Papaver
nudicaule*

*Papaver
orientale*

*Passiflora
edulis*

*Pelargonium
peltatum*

The oriental poppies are derived from *P. orientale*, a sturdy, leafy plant with large scarlet flowers blotched with black within. They appear in June. White and pink varieties have also been produced and some with fringed petals, They like sunny places and well-drained soils and can be raised from seed sown out-doors in May or by root cuttings in winter. Seedlings may vary a little from their parents.

The Iceland poppy *P. nudicaule*, though a perennial, is usually grown either as an annual or as a biennial, seed being sown in a greenhouse in February or March and the seedlings planted out in May for July and August flowering, or sown in a greenhouse or frame in June to be planted out in August or September for flowering early next summer. They need a sunny place and well-drained soil. The flowers are very dainty, carried on slender but firm stems, 12 to 18 inches high, and the colour range includes yellow, pink, orange and tangerine.

PASSIFLORA *(Passion Flower)*

These are vigorous climbing plants many of which are too tender to be grown outdoors in this country. *Passiflora caerulea*, how-ever, will succeed on warm and sheltered walls where it will soon make a mass of growth extending to 15 or 20 feet and freely cov-ered in late summer with remarkable pale blue, white and purple flowers. There is a pure white variety named Constance Elliott.

P. edulis, sometimes known as the purple grenadilla, has white and purple flowers followed by large, egg-shaped fruits which are edible. *P. antioquiensis (Van Volxemii)* also has edible fruits and very showy, scarlet flowers. Both these must be grown in a warm greenhouse.

All passion flowers are readily and quickly raised from seed sown in a warm greenhouse in spring. They like good, loamy soils and plenty of sun.

PELARGONIUM *(Geranium)*

This is one of those flowers the nomenclature of which has become very confused in gardens. What everyone calls geranium is, in fact, a pelargonium, and the true geraniums are hardy herbaceous plants which are not often seen though several of them are well worth growing.

The pelargoniums may conveniently be considered in three groups—the popular zonal-leaved varieties so largely used for summer bedding, the ivy-leaved pelargoniums popular for window boxes, hanging baskets, etc., and the show or regal pelargoniums grown as pot plants for the greenhouse.

Best known of the zonal-leaved varieties is the scarlet flowered Paul Crampel, but there are newer and better varieties such as the semi-double Gustav Emich. There are also varieties with white, pink and carmine flowers and a number with variegated leaves. All are bushy plants which will flower all the summer outdoors, or most of the winter under glass if the summer buds are picked off. All like sun and warmth and will grow in almost any soil. They can be increased by cuttings of firm young growth

96

Polygonatum multiflorum

imula lyantha

nus serrulata 'Kanzan'

Phyteuma Scheuchzeri

Platycodon grandiflorum

Primula malacoides

Polygonum affine

Potentilla fruticosa

Plumbago capensis

Polemonium caeruleum

Pulmonaria officinalis

Pyracantha coccinea Lalandii

CNT

Rosa [Floribunda type]

Rhus typhina

Rudbeckia speciosa

Ramonda Myconi

Romneya Coulteri

Rosa Moyesii

Rodgersia pinnata

Reseda odorata

Rhododendron ponticum

Ribes sanguineum

Ranunculus asiaticus

Saintpaulia ionantha

Rosmarinus officinalis

CNF

in a frame in late summer or a warm greenhouse in spring.

The ivy-leaved pelargoniums are grown in exactly the same way except that they are trailing plants which can be allowed to fall over the edge of something, be tied up to a stake or other support, or simply be allowed to sprawl over the ground. The popular varieties nearly all have pink, double flowers, but there are also red varieties.

The show and regal pelargoniums are bushy plants not unlike the zonals in habit but they have much larger flowers usually pink more or less heavily blotched with crimson or maroon. They flower in late spring and early summer and are grown as pot plants in moderately heated greenhouses, usually being stood outside or in a frame during July and August to rest. In other respects their treatment is as for zonal pelargoniums.

Pelargonium denticulatum

PENSTEMON *(Beard Tongue)*

There are dwarf, more or less shrubby penstemons such as *Penstemon rupicola*, *P. heterophyllus* and *P. Scouleri* which can be grown in the rock garden, but the most popular are the many large-flowered kinds collectively known as *P. gloxinoides* and distinguished by fancy names such as Newbury Gem and Garnet. Some are not quite hardy and may need the protection of a frame in winter, but others are quite hardy in many parts of the country. They grow about 2 feet high and have spikes of fine tubular flowers, the general effect at a short distance being not unlike that of antirrhinums. Colours range from white through pink to scarlet and purple and the flowering season from June to October. All like sun though they will put up with some shade. They are not fussy about soil and can be readily increased by cuttings of non-flowering shoots in a frame in August or September.

Pelargonium zonale

PERNETTYA *(Prickly Heath)*

The only kind much grown in gardens, *Pernettya mucronata*, is a freely branching evergreen shrub 2 or 3 feet high with neat glossy green leaves, small white flowers in May, followed by large berries in the most remarkable colours, bright rose pink, lilac, purple, red, crimson, near black and white. This is a first-class dwarf shrub for rather moist and cool peaty or leafy soils. It likes sun and requires no pruning. As it suckers very freely it can be increased by detaching these with roots in autumn or early spring. It can also be raised from seeds sown in a frame in spring.

Penstemon heterophyllus

PEROVSKIA

Only one kind is commonly cultivated, *Perovskia atriplicifolia*, a shrub that is apt to be killed to near ground level each winter and then throws up a number of straight 4-foot stems bearing small grey leaves, and, on the upper half, small lavender blue flowers. The whole effect in August is extremely charming, a grey-lavender mist of colour. This is a shrub for the sunniest places and the best drained soils, but not poor soils. It resents

Pernettya mucronata

G

97

*Petunia
axillaris*

*Philadelphus
grandiflorus*

*Philadelphus
coronarius*

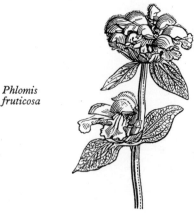

*Phlomis
fruticosa*

root disturbance and should be raised in pots so that it can be planted with the minimum of damage. It is best propagated by root cuttings in winter.

PETUNIA

These popular half-hardy annuals have been greatly developed as summer bedding plants. For this purpose very free-flowering varieties, with flowers of medium size and usually of one colour throughout, are preferred to the larger flowered and usually striped or blotched varieties of former years. Double-flowered varieties are also available.

All can be raised from seed sown in a warm greenhouse in February or March. Seedlings must be pricked out and hardened off for planting outdoors in late May or early June. Petunias like sun, warmth and good drainage and are not so happy on cold, wet soils. Most modern bedding varieties grow about 1 foot high. The colour range is in blue, violet, purple, pink, rose, crimson and white.

PHACELIA

The most popular phacelia in Britain is *Phacelia campanularia*, a very attractive hardy annual 6 to 8 inches high, spreading in habit, with flowers of the clearest possible blue. There are other annual species such as *P. minor*, *P. Whitlavii* and *P. viscida*, but *P. campanularia* is the best. All can be grown from seed sown outdoors in April where the plants are to flower in July. A sunny position and well-drained soil should be chosen for preference and the seedlings should be thinned to 6 or 8 inches.

PHILADELPHUS   *(Mock Orange)*

The mock oranges are free flowering shrubs with white flowers in June or July and many are extremely fragrant. They grow vigorously in almost all soils and are not in the least difficult. They prefer sunny positions and need no regular pruning but, if desired, to reduce the size of the bushes, flowering stems can be removed as soon as the flowers fade.

There are many kinds some being hybrids known as *Philadelphus Lemoinei* and having names such as Virginal, Belle Étoile, and Beauclerk. Some have single, some double flowers and heights vary from about 4 to 8 feet. There are also some good species, notably *P. coronarius*, 8 to 10 feet high with single, very fragrant flowers; *P. grandiflorus*, large flowered but scentless, and *P. microphyllus*, no more than 5 feet high with exceptionally fragrant, rather starry flowers. *P. purpureo-maculatus* is a hybrid with single white flowers carrying a purple blotch at the base of each petal. All can be increased by cuttings of firm young stems in autumn.

PHLOMIS   *(Jerusalem Sage)*

The common Jerusalem Sage, *Phlomis fruticosa*, is a grey-leaved shrub with rather soft, sappy shoots which are all the better for a little pruning to keep them as stiff as possible. The whorls of fine, yellow, sage-like flowers are produced in June or July and as soon as they fade the flowering stems can be shortened a little. The bush grows about 3 feet high but tends to flop and spread. It is an attractive plant for a warm sunny place and even if it is cut back by frost in winter it usually breaks away strongly from the base next spring. It can be increased by cuttings of firm young shoots in summer in a propagating frame.

PHLOX

There are phloxes for the herbaceous border and phloxes for the rock garden or dry wall and all are useful, easily grown plants. The border phloxes are mostly derived from *Phlox paniculata* (*decussata*) and there are a great many varieties designated by fancy names such as Brigadier, Border Gem, Frau Antonia Buchner, Sweetheart and Mrs Ethel Prichard. All flower in July or August and have fine trusses of fragrant flowers, the colour range being from white and palest pink or mauve to scarlet, crimson and violet. They are grand plants for sunny or partially shaded places in good, rich soil which does not dry out too rapidly. Heights vary from about 2 to 5 feet and all can be increased by division in spring or autumn or by root cuttings in winter.

Among the best of the rock garden phloxes are the many varieties derived from *P. subulata*, sometimes known as the moss pink. These are mat-forming plants with narrow leaves and almost stemless rose-pink, lilac, mauve or white flowers in May and June. All can be increased by summer cuttings in a frame.

PHYGELIUS   (*Cape Fuchsia*)

The Cape fuchsia, *Phygelius capensis*, is an interesting and attractive perennial with 4-foot high stems bearing in summer curved, tubular flowers that are a brilliant orange-scarlet. It is hardy enough for a great many parts of the country but it likes a warm, sunny spot and a fairly well-drained soil. It can be very readily increased by division in the spring.

PHYTEUMA   (*Horned Rampion*)

These are very attractive rock plants with curiously formed flowers which at a short distance look rather like little bladders terminating in a tiny horn or spike. These are usually blue or white, and are produced in late spring or early summer. Very typical of the family and one of the best to grow is *Phyteuma comosum* which makes a low, spreading clump 4 to 6 inches high with purple and lilac flowers. Other good kinds are *P. Scheuchzeri*, and *P. orbiculare*, blue, 1 foot; and *P. hemisphaericum*, blue, 3 to 4 inches. All like sunny places and well-drained soils and all can be increased either by division in spring or by seed sown in a frame at the same season.

PLATYCODON   (*Balloon Flower*)

Only one kind of platycodon is grown in gardens but it has several varieties. It is a hardy herbaceous plant named *Platycodon*

Phlox
Drummondii

Phlox
procumbens

Phlox
paniculata

Phyteuma
orbiculare

*Platycodon
grandiflorum*

*Plumbago
capensis*

*Polemonium
caeruleum*

*Polygonatum
officinale*

grandiflorum and it flowers in July and August. It grows 12 to 18 inches high and has bell shaped light blue flowers which are very similar to those of some campanulas. It is in bud that the plant is most striking for the buds are large and inflated like so many small, blue balloons. This is a good and slightly unusual plant for a sunny place and a good, loamy soil. There are varieties with white flowers and one, named *Mariesii*, which is rather dwarfer than most and has blue flowers of deeper colour and greater size. All are readily increased by division in spring.

PLUMBAGO (Leadwort)

Plumbago capensis is a beautiful and easily grown greenhouse climber with trusses of pale blue, phlox-like flowers in summer. It is a perennial and is best planted directly in the greenhouse border though it can be grown in a tub or large pot. It likes good loamy soil and plenty of water in summer. It should be trained around a pillar or to wires strained beneath the rafters and may be kept to moderate dimensions by cutting back all the previous year's shoots to 8 or 9 inches each March. Only enough heat is required in winter to keep out frost. Increase by cuttings taken with a heel in April and rooted in a propagating frame.

POLEMONIUM (Jacob's Ladder)

These are hardy herbaceous perennials, the only one of which at all commonly seen in gardens is *Polemonium caeruleum*. It is called Jacob's ladder because of the ladder-like appearance of its pinnate leaves. The blue flowers are carried in short spikes on foot-high stems in early summer and are as freely produced in partial shade as they are in full sun. This is, in fact, a very easy plant to grow in almost any soil and position and used to be a great favourite in cottage gardens. It is easily increased by division in either spring or autumn.

POLYGONATUM (Solomon's Seal)

The best known and most generally useful of this family is *Polygonatum multiflorum*. It is a graceful plant making arching stems reaching a height of about 3 feet and bearing smooth grey-ish green leaves which are themselves decorative. In May and June tubular creamy white flowers hang downwards along the upper half of these stems. It is the curious seal-like marks on the tubers that have suggested the popular name Solomon's seal. This plant likes cool, leafy, rather moist soils and partially shaded positions and may be naturalized in thin woodland. It is also first rate in shady borders. It can be increased very readily by division in spring or autumn.

POLYGONUM (Knotweed)

Some of the knotweeds really are weeds of the most obnoxious kind, penetrating far and wide and, once admitted to the garden, not easily dismissed from it again. But among them are some useful and entirely safe garden plants. Two of the best of these are

Saxifraga Burseriana

Sedum
spurium

Saxifraga
umbrosa

ponaria
ccaria

Salvia
splendens

Schizanthus
hybridus

Salpiglossis
sinuata

Scabiosa
caucasica

Sanguisorba
obtusa

Scilla
hispanica

Santolina
Chamaecyparissus

Salvia patens

Saxifraga
[mossy hybrid]

Spiraea Vanhouttei

Solidago
canadensis

Spartium
junceum

Silene
Schafta

Sisyrinchium
angustifolium

Sempervivum
calcareum

Sidalcea
malvaeflora

Solanum
jasminoides
album

Stachys
lanata

Senecio
laxifolius

Strelitzia
Reginae

Skimmia
japonica

Shortia
uniflora
grandiflora

CN

trailers for the rock garden or dry wall, *Polygonum affine* and *P. vaccinifolium*. Both make carpets of growth from which arise in late summer and early autumn dainty spikes of pink flowers. *P. vaccinifolium* is the smaller and neater of the two, but *P. affine* scores in having fine autumn foliage effects as an additional attraction. Two kinds for the herbaceous border are *P. Bistorta sanguineum* and *P. campanulatum*, the first with slender spikes of deep red flowers on 2–foot stems and the second with small sprays of pale pink flowers on 3–foot stems. Both flower without break from July to October and both are easy to grow in almost any position but *P. campanulatum* needs plenty of moisture in summer. All these knotweeds can be increased by division in spring or autumn. *Polygonum baldschuanicum* is a rampant climber with white, pink tinged flowers from July to October. It is useful for covering sheds, fences, pergolas and walls.

Polygonum
Bistorta

POTENTILLA *(Cinquefoil)*

The potentillas are fine plants for rather dry, sunny places. They do not seem to mind how poor the soil is, indeed they usually flower more freely when it is rather poor. Most are hardy herbaceous perennials, some, such as *Potentilla nitida*, with silvery leaves and pink flowers, and *P. nepalensis* with cherry red flowers, being small enough for the rock garden, and others, such as the numerous varieties of *P. atro sanguinea* being better suited to the herbaceous border. *P. atro sanguinea* itself has single scarlet flowers but there are other forms which are double or semi-double and range in colour from yellow through orange and scarlet to crimson. All are about 18 inches in height with the exception of Gibson's Scarlet which is almost prostrate, and all flower from June to August. Division in spring or autumn is the simplest method of increasing all these potentillas. *P. fruticosa* is a shrubby species which grows up to 4 feet high. It has yellow flowers borne in summer and there are many beautiful varieties with flowers larger and deeper in colour or paler than the type.

Potentilla
nitida

PRIMULA *(Primrose, Polyanthus, Auricula)*

A number of most popular hardy and greenhouse plants are to be found in this family. Our native primrose is *Primula vulgaris* and this has given rise not only to many coloured garden forms but also, with the cowslip, to the multi-flowered polyanthus (*P. polyantha*). There are all shades of pink, yellow, orange, scarlet, crimson and blue and there are double-flowered forms of the primrose as well as the more familiar singles. They are plants for rather good, loamy or leafy soils and cool perhaps partially shaded positions, and all can be increased either by careful division after flowering or by seed sown in spring in a frame.

The popular auricula is botanically *P. Auricula*, a plant with rather leathery leaves, more or less heavily dusted with grey meal, and clusters of brightly coloured flowers in spring on 8–inch stems. It has been greatly developed in gardens and there are many different colours.

Primula
Auricula

Primula
cortusoides

101

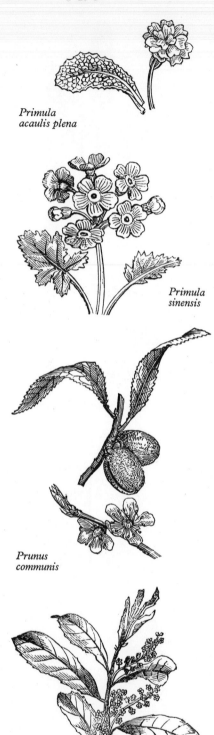

Primula
acaulis plena

Primula
sinensis

Prunus
communis

Prunus
Laurocerasus

Then there are a great many primulas for the rock garden, some with flowers in round clusters such as the pale blue *P. denticulata* or violet *P. capitata*, some with flowers in loose heads, such as the pink *P. frondosa*, bright rose *P. rosea* and lilac *P. Edgeworthii*, some almost stemless such as the wine coloured *P. Juliae* and at least one, *P. Vialii*, with its purple flowers in spikes. Most of these like cool, rather leafy or peaty soils.

There is another group of hardy primulas that is happiest in the bog garden or at the side of a pool or stream. The yellow flowered *P. Florindae* and *P. helodoxa* and magenta *P. japonica* and *P. pulverulenta* are of this type and they are vigorous plants growing 2 to 4 feet in height and often renewing themselves by seed where conditions suit them.

Finally there are the greenhouse primulas of which *P. obconica*, *P. sinensis* and *P. malacoides* are the best known examples. All these have numerous garden varieties differing in colour and size and form of flower and all flower in winter. They should be renewed annually from seed sown in April for *P. sinensis* and *P. obconica* and in June for *P. malacoides*. The seedlings are grown on singly in small pots, being moved on as they require it and usually flowered in the 5-inch size. Very little heat is needed, just enough to prevent the temperature from falling below 45°.

PRUNUS *(Cherry, Plum, Peach, Almond)*

Some of the best ornamental trees of moderate size are to be found in this family. The Japanese cherries derived from *Prunus Lannesiana* and *P. serrulata* are particularly good. They have a considerable range of habit from the erect Amanogawa, with branches ascending like those of a Lombardy poplar to the spreading Fugenzo which when fully grown may cover 30 feet or more of ground. Colours range from white and bluish pink to quite a warm pink and there are single and double-flowered forms. All flower in April or early May. Then there is the lovely autumn-flowering *Prunus subhirtella autumnalis* with small but abundant white or shell-pink flowers and the weeping form of *P. subhirtella* which flowers in spring. *P. yedoensis* is white-flowered and exceptionally free in March and April and *P. Sargentii* has pink flowers at the same season and foliage which is bronze in spring and orange-scarlet in autumn. These are all cherries.

Among the plums the two best are the popular purple-leaved *P. cerasifera Pissardii* which produces its small pale pink flowers in February and March and *P. cerasifera Blireana* which has larger, deeper pink semi-double flowers.

The ornamental peaches are all varieties of *P. persica*. One of the best, Clara Meyer, has very double rose-pink flowers in April. Iceberg is a pure white and Russell's Red a good carmine.

The almonds flower a week or so earlier than the peaches and the commonest kind, *P. communis (Amygdalus)*, is also the best.

The common cherry laurel used for hedging is *P. Laurocerasus*.

One other prunus which merits special mention is *P. triloba flore pleno*. The young branches of this are wreathed in very double pink flowers each April but it is a little more tender than

most and really needs a warm sheltered wall. It is often grown
as a pot plant in a cool greenhouse.

All these prunus like good, loamy soils and sunny positions.
They need no regular pruning. Increase by budding in summer.

PULMONARIA *(Lungwort)*

The lungworts, useful hardy perennials because they flower
very early, will grow well in partial shade and several have distinctly decorative foliage. This is particularly true of *P. officinalis*
and *P. saccharata*, both of which have green leaves spotted with
white. Their flowers are red fading to purple. Better from the
point of view of flowers is *P. angustifolia* with clear blue flowers.
All are quite dwarf plants for the front of the border and all will
grow in any reasonable soil. They can be increased by division
in spring or autumn.

PYRACANTHA *(Firethorn)*

These are evergreen shrubs naturally bushy and branching in
habit but often trained against walls. For this *Pyracantha coccinea*,
with clusters of small white flowers in early June followed by
scarlet berries in autumn is often used. It has a very fine form
named *Lalandii* in which the berries are larger and of a more
orange-scarlet. Then there is *P. Gibbsii* with smaller, deep red
berries produced with even greater profusion, and *P. Rogersiana
fructu luteo* which has yellow berries.

All these like good loamy soils but may be grown almost anywhere. They will thrive in sun or shade and are excellent for
clothing north walls. Pyracanthas are increased by seeds sown
in spring or by cuttings made from side shoots pulled off with a
heel in July or August and rooted in a propagating frame. When
grown as bushes they need not be pruned but when trained
against a wall it will be necessary to cut back badly placed side
shoots each summer.

RAMONDA

The ramondas are those rather rare things, rock plants that
prefer shade to sun. They make flat rosettes of rather leathery
leaves that like to press themselves flat against the face of a ver-
tical crevice in a wall or between large stones. But for them to be
perfectly happy the crevice should face north. The flowers, which
are not unlike those of a potato in form, are produced in twos
or threes on 6–inch stems in May and June. They are soft bluish
lilac in the popular *Ramonda pyrenaica (Myconi)*, but there is
also a white-flowered form of this and one that is not far removed from clear pink. *R. Nathaliae* has bluer flowers and is
very attractive. All like cool, peaty or leafy soils and can be
raised from seeds sown in a frame in March or by leaf cuttings
in early summer.

RANUNCULUS *(Buttercup, Fair Maids of France)*

No one wants to cultivate common buttercups, pretty though
they are, but the ranunculus family is a large one and contains

*Pulmonaria (Mertensia)
virginica*

*Pulmonaria
officinalis*

*Pyracantha
coccinea*

*Ramonda
pyrenaica*

*Ranunculus
aconitifolius*

*Reseda
odorata*

*Rhododendron
ponticum*

*Rhododendron
Thomsonii*

many species very different from the yellow weeds of our meadows and lawns. One of the most striking of these is *Ranunculus asiaticus*, familiarly known as the turban ranunculus. The garden forms of this always have fully double flowers like brightly coloured balls, some yellow, some scarlet, some crimson, all beautiful. They are carried on 9–inch stems in May and June and are excellent for cutting. The plants have small tuberous roots which should be planted 2 inches deep in good loamy soil and a warm sunny position. If the soil is really well drained they can be planted in November but in damp, cold places it is better to wait until late February or early March. In July the tubers should be lifted carefully and stored in a cool dry place until planting time. *R. aconitifolius* is a white flowered hardy perennial, loveliest in its double form.

RESEDA *(Mignonette)*

The mignonette, *Reseda odorata*, is one of the most pleasantly fragrant of annuals and though its broad spikes of small, pale green and red flowers are not showy, they make a pleasant change in the annual border from the more brightly coloured plants. It is a hardy annual, seed of which should be sown in March, April or early May where it is to flower. The seedlings should be thinned to 6 or 8 inches. Mignonette likes sunny places and is not fussy about soil though many gardeners believe that it does best where there is chalk. It can also be grown in pots as a greenhouse plant.

RHODODENDRON

This is one of those huge families about which it is difficult to generalize without being completely misleading. All rhododendrons are shrubs but some are so small that they can be grown quite easily in the rock garden and some are so big that they appear like trees. The shrubs commonly known as azaleas are, in fact, rhododendrons but for the sake of clarity they have been kept separate in this book.

All the rhododendrons with which we are concerned here are evergreen and almost all dislike limy or chalky soils. They like peat or leaf mould though this is not essential to them and they will grow well in any loamy soil that is not alkaline. There are hundreds of species some, such as *Rhododendron impeditum* and *R. racemosum*, with quite small flowers, while others such as *R. Griffithianum* and *R. Falconeri* have very large flowers. In addition there are great numbers of garden hybrids many of which are hardier and easier to grow than the species though they may lack some of their grace. The peak flowering period for these hybrids is May and early June and most make big, rounded bushes with handsome leaves and fine trusses of bloom. Colours range from white and pale pink to scarlet, crimson and purple.

Rhododendrons are easy to transplant and are best obtained in autumn or early spring. Most prefer a little shade and are happiest in thin woodland, but many of the hardy hybrids will also grow well in full sun. All benefit from an annual top dressing of peat or leaf mould which may be applied in spring or autumn.

Most of the good hybrids are increased by grafting in a warm greenhouse in spring, *R. ponticum* usually being used as a stock, but even better plants can be raised from layers pegged down in early summer. They may take 18 months or more to form roots.

RHUS *(Sumach)*

Several of the shrubs formerly known as rhus have now been transferred to another genus named Cotinus where they will be found in this book. Here we are principally concerned with the stag's-horn sumach, *Rhus typhina*, a handsome small tree with long, pinnate leaves which turn scarlet or crimson before falling in autumn. The fruits are also curious and beautiful— erect conglomerations of tiny crimson fruitlets which look a little like red horns and presumably have suggested the popular name. A variety of this has leaves so much divided that they look almost like the fronds of a fern. This sumach will grow in any ordinary soil and open position. It reaches a height of about 12 feet and suckers freely. These suckers, detached in autumn with some root, provide a ready means of increase.

RIBES *(Currant)*

Most of the currants are utilitarian rather than ornamental but the American currant, *Ribes sanguineum*, is a showy early flowering shrub with short trails of rose pink flowers in March and April. It makes a big, dense bush as much as 8 feet high and it has numerous varieties, some with pale flowers and some deep carmine. Two of the best of these are King Edward VII and Pulborough Scarlet. All are very easily grown in practically any soil and sunny or partially shaded position. They can be readily increased by cuttings of firm young shoots in the autumn.

RODGERSIA

These very attractive hardy perennials have handsome leaves and branched sprays of small flowers a little like those of some spiraeas. They like damp places but will also grow quite well in ordinary soil provided it does not dry out too severely.

One of the best kinds is *Rodgersia pinnata* the leaves of which are made up of several separate leaflets. The flowers are rose pink and carried on 3 to 4–foot stems in July. *R. tabularis* has larger, undivided leaves not unlike those of some ornamental rhubarbs and the flowers are white. All can be increased by division in spring or autumn.

ROMNEYA *(Californian Tree Poppy)*

This is one of those plants that is not quite a shrub and yet not quite a herbaceous plant either. It makes a woody crown from which are thrown up each year 6–foot cane-like stems carrying blue-grey leaves and terminated in summer by a succession of large white poppies each with a central boss of golden stamens. In winter these stems usually die down to the base again to be replaced by a new crop the following year. The Californian tree

Rhododendron arboreum

Rhododendron caucasicum

Rhododendron maximum

Ribes sanguineum

*Rosa chinensis
flore pleno*

*Rosa
Banksiae*

*Rosa
bracteata*

*Rosa
centifolia*

poppy, a beautiful plant for rather poor, stony soils and sunny positions, is hardy in most parts of the country but does not survive bad drainage and dislikes cold, wet soils. It is difficult to transplant and a start should be made with small plants from pots so that they can be transferred to the ground with a minimum of root disturbance. Propagation is by root cuttings in winter.

The kind usually grown is *Romneya Coulteri*, but *R. trichocalyx* is sometimes seen. They are very similar.

ROSA (Rose)

The rose is the most highly developed of all flowers. It has been bred and hybridized for centuries and, as a result, it has developed an immense variety of forms, colours and habits.

To-day the most popular classes of rose for garden display are the hybrid teas, the floribundas, the dwarf polyanthas, the hybrid musks, the climbing roses mainly of H.T. origin and the ramblers mainly derived from *Rosa Wichuraiana* and *R. multiflora*.

The hybrid teas are bush roses usually 2 to 4 feet in height and mostly with large double flowers, though a few singles are still grown. They flower throughout the summer with a main flush of bloom in June and early July and a secondary peak in September. The colour range includes practically everything except blue and many new varieties are added to the list every year.

The floribundas are mainly derived from the roses once known as hybrid polyanthas. They are also bush roses similar to the H.T.s in habit though usually a little more vigorous and freely branched. Their flowers are of medium size, usually produced in fine clusters, and their flowering season is similar to that of the H.T.s. They are the bedding roses *par excellence* to-day.

The dwarf polyanthas are bush roses usually of more dwarf and compact habit. Their flowers are quite small, like those of rambler roses, and are similarly produced in large clusters. They flower continuously throughout the summer.

The hybrid musks look very much like the floribundas but on the whole make even larger bushes, some of them reaching a height of 7 or 8 feet. Their flowers are small to medium, produced in big clusters and though they are all-summer flowering they are particularly good in the autumn.

The climbing roses grow to a height of 10 or 12 feet and mostly have rather large flowers similar to those of the H.T.s from which many of them are derived. They do well trained against walls or on pillars and they have a fairly long season in bloom.

The rambler roses are much more vigorous, often reaching a height of 15 feet or more, and their flowers, though small, are produced in very large clusters. Most of them flower in June or July and do not give any earlier or later display. These are the best roses for covering pergolas or large screens.

In addition there are miniature roses growing no more than 6 or 8 inches high and a great many other classes some so old

106

that they have almost been forgotten. The rose species, too, provide valuable material for the shrub border and some, such as *Rosa Moyesii*, are worth growing for their scarlet heps as well as for their flowers.

All roses like good loamy soils. They thrive best in sunny places though a few kinds, such as the rambler Alberic Barbier and climber Mermaid, will succeed in shade. All are best planted in autumn though they can be moved at any time between October and April. Pruning must be varied to suit particular varieties and this is a subject which must be left for specialist books. Propagation is usually either by cuttings of firm young stems in autumn or by budding in July.

ROSMARINUS *(Rosemary)*

The common rosemary, *Rosmarinus officinalis*, is a delightful evergreen shrub, usually 4 to 5 feet high, with narrow aromatic leaves and small, pale blue flowers in May. It is a little tender and apt to be damaged by severe frost or cold winds, but can be grown outdoors in most parts of the country. It likes good but well-drained soils and warm, sunny places and needs no regular pruning. Propagation is by cuttings of firm young shoots in a frame in July or August. There are numerous varieties, one with white flowers and several with flowers of a deeper blue. The completely prostrate rosemary often known as *R. prostratus* is really *R. lavendulaceus* and is much less hardy than the common rosemary.

RUDBECKIA *(Coneflower)*

These are hardy herbaceous and hardy annual plants very closely related to the sunflowers and looking much like them. In several kinds the central disk is raised and cone-shaped instead of being flat, hence the popular name coneflower. Three of the best perennial kinds are *Rudbeckia speciosa* (*Newmannii*) 2 to 3 feet high with orange yellow, black-centred flowers; *R. nitida* Herbstonne, 6 or 7 feet high with bright yellow, green-centred flowers, and *R. laciniata* Golden Glow, 7 to 8 feet tall, with double yellow flowers. All flower in August and September.

Best of the annual rudbeckias is *R. hirta* which grows about 2 feet high and has yellow flowers. There are a number of hybrids of this with a colour range from yellow to deep chestnut red. All are readily grown from seed sown in April where the plants are to flower. Seedlings should be thinned to a least a foot apart.

SAINTPAULIA *(South African Violet)*

The only species grown in gardens is *Saintpaulia ionantha* but this is a variable plant and it has produced a number of varieties. Typically it is a low growing greenhouse perennial with soft, velvety green leaves and violet blue flowers carried in small clusters on 6-inch stems. In a warm greenhouse it will go on flowering almost the entire year. The varieties differ mainly in colour, from near white to pink and deepest violet, but there

107

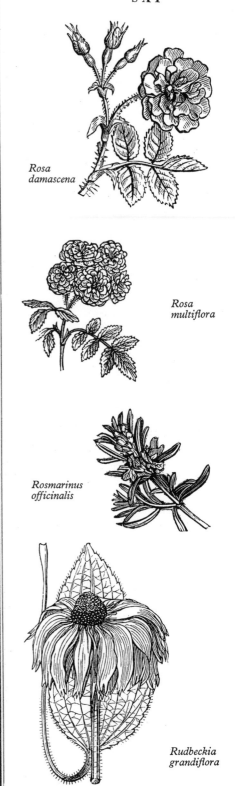

Rosa damascena

Rosa multiflora

Rosmarinus officinalis

Rudbeckia grandiflora

*Salpiglossis
sinuata*

*Salvia
splendens*

*Salvia
Grahamii*

*Salvia
patens*

are also some double flowered forms. All like a compost with plenty of peat or good leaf mould and thrive best in a fairly warm moist greenhouse. A minimum winter temperature of around 55° rising to 65° in summer suits them admirably. They will grow equally well in sun or shade, should be watered freely in summer and moderately in winter and may be raised from seed in February, by careful division in March or April, or by leaf cuttings in summer.

SALPIGLOSSIS

These lovely plants are not the easiest of half-hardy annuals to grow well. Their trumpet shaped blooms are carried all summer on stems 3 feet in height and are usually purple, rose, scarlet, cream or rose, in many cases veined with gold. The effect is delightful and the salpiglossis is worth a little trouble. Seed should be sown in a moderately heated greenhouse in February or March and the seedlings either pricked out and hardened off, if they are to be flowered out of doors, or potted singly if they are to be grown in pots for the greenhouse. Outdoors they should be given a warm sunny position and good but well-drained soil. Plant at the end of May or early in June and space at least 1 foot apart. In the greenhouse they can be flowered in 5- or 6-inch pots and should be grown in John Innes compost.

SALVIA *(Sage)*

The common sage, *Salvia officinalis*, though primarily a herb, is in its variegated forms not a plant to be despised in the ornamental garden. There are, however, many other purely ornamental kinds of salvia, some hardy plants for the herbaceous border, some half-hardy plants for summer bedding and several poised rather uneasily both between hardiness and tenderness and between a shrubby and a herbaceous habit. An example of this last class is *Salvia Grahamii*, a rather softly shrubby plant 3 feet in height, which produces scarlet flowers in constant succession from July to October if only one can find a place warm enough to suit it.

Far more generally useful and much more popular is the genuinely half-hardy *S. splendens*, the familiar scarlet salvia of summer bedding schemes. This can be treated as a half-hardy annual if seed is sown in a warm greenhouse in January or early February, the seedlings being potted singly and hardened off for planting out in early June. Alternatively cuttings can be rooted in a warm greenhouse between January and March and treated in a similar manner. A plant that loves sunny places and does best in warm summers, it grows 18 to 24 inches high and produces its abundant spikes of vivid scarlet flowers from July until the first autumn frost.

Best of the hardy herbaceous salvias is that usually known in gardens as *S. virgata nemorosa* though its correct name is *S. superba*. It grows about 3 feet high and produces its slender purple spikes in July and August. It is quite hardy, very easily grown in any ordinary soil and open position and is certainly one of the

Syringa vulgaris [garden form]

Streptocarpus hybridus

Thalictrum dipterocarpum

Tigridia Pavonia

Symphoricarpos racemosus

Trollius europaeus

Tamarix pentandra

Tagetes patula [garden form]

Trillium grandiflorum

...mus Serpyllum

Tropaeolum majus

Tradescantia virginiana

Wisteria
sinensis

Viola
tricolor
[pansy]

Weigela
florida

Vinca
minor

Venidium
fastuosum

Tulipa
Gesneriana
[garden
form]

Verbascum
Brousa

Veroni
spicata

Zinnia elegans
[garden form]

Yucca
filamentosa

Viburnum
Carlesii

Verbena
venosa

Viburnum
Opulus

CN-T

best dozen or so border plants. *S. Sclarea* and its variety *turkestanica* are worth growing for their large, hairy leaves as well as for their 3–foot spikes of pale blue or pinkish flowers, and *S. uliginosa* is one of the truest blue flowers of late summer. Finally there is the tuberous rooted *S. patens* which has gentian blue flowers in summer but is not entirely hardy and may need to be lifted and placed in a frame for the winter.

SANGUISORBA *(Burnet)*

The plants which the botanist calls sanguisorba the gardener very often calls poterium and in nursery catalogues they are as likely to be found under the one name as the other. The two best are *Sanguisorba canadensis* and *S. obtusa*, the first with bottle-brush spikes of fluffy white flowers and the second similar in style but pink in colour. Both flower in August and September and are hardy herbaceous perennials. They like sunny places and can be increased by division in the spring.

SANTOLINA *(Lavender Cotton)*

The lavender cottons are technically shrubs but they are comparatively soft-stemmed and low-growing and are usually grown in the herbaceous border, frequently as edgings in the manner of lavender or catmint. The most popular, *Santolina Chamaecyparissus*, has tiny silvery leaves and grows 18 to 24 inches high. It has yellow, tansy-like flowers in summer, but it is grown for its silver foliage rather than for these. It can be increased by careful division in the autumn or by cuttings of firm young shoots taken in July and rooted in a propagating frame.

SAPONARIA *(Soapwort)*

The common soapwort, *Saponaria officinalis*, is a hardy herbaceous plant 18 to 24 inches high with heads of pink flowers in August and September. It is usually seen in its double flowered form and is a showy though somewhat coarse plant. Perhaps more generally useful is the sprawling and trailing *S. ocymoides*, a fine plant for a steep bank or a dry wall. It will quickly cover several square feet of space with its loose mounds of growth which disappear in June and July beneath a cloud of small pink flowers.

Both these plants are perennials. There is also a useful annual kind, *S. Vaccaria*, which makes slender 18-inch stems carrying very dainty pink or white flowers that are excellent for cutting. It can be raised from seed sown in March, April or May where the plants are to flower.

All these like sunny places and all thrive in any ordinary soil. *S. officinalis* can be increased by division in spring, *S. ocymoides* by seed in a frame or greenhouse in spring.

SAXIFRAGA *(Saxifrage)*

This is one of the great families of rock garden plants and there are so many different kinds that it is necessary to consider them in their respective groups rather than as individuals.

First to flower are the cushion or Kabschia saxifrages, all of

109

Sanguisorba officinalis

Santolina neopolitana

Saponaria officinalis

Saxifraga Cotyledon

*Saxifraga
muscoides*

*Saxifraga
sarmentosa*

*Saxifraga
hypnoides*

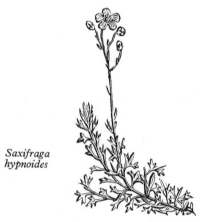

*Saxifraga
Geum*

which make compact hummocks of growth from which the flowers are produced in March and April, usually on short stems
though some kinds appear almost stemless. There are white,
yellow and pink kinds and all are beautiful. These are plants for
sunny places in the rock garden in really well-drained soil which
may contain as much as 50% of stone chippings. Because of their
habit of flowering very early, many gardeners grow them in
pans and allow them to bloom under glass so that they are not
spoiled by the weather. Fine examples of this group are *Saxifraga Burseriana*, white, and *S. Cranbourne*, pink.

Next come the silver saxifrages which make fine rosettes of
firm-textured leaves often heavily silvered along the margins.
Their flowers are borne in loose clusters which are often of considerable size. The commonest colour is white, sometimes
speckled with red as in the popular *S. Cotyledon caterhamensis*,
but there are yellow and pink varieties. All like to grow in crevices between rocks or between stones in a dry wall. The position
should be open and sunny.

By contrast the mossy saxifrages like cool, rather moist soils
and partially shaded positions. They make soft mounds of
bright green leaves and flower in May, the flowers varying considerably both in size and in the length of the stems on which
they are borne. White, pink and red are the commonest colours
in this group. Two fine examples are *S. Wallacei* and *S. hypnoides*.

The familiar London pride is a saxifrage belonging to yet
another group. Its name is *S. umbrosa* and it makes rosettes of
green leaves bearing in May and June, loose sprays of small pink
flowers. It will grow practically anywhere in sun or shade.

In addition to these there are saxifrages, such as *S. Griesbachii*,
which make silver rosettes of leaves from which ascend flowering
stems clothed in crimson bracts, and saxifrages such as *S. opposi-
tifolia* which lie flat on the ground and carry their flowers stemless on this carpet.

Almost all saxifrages can be increased by careful division after
flowering and many can also be raised from seed sown in a frame
or greenhouse in spring.

SCABIOSA *(Scabious)*

There are a number of species of scabious but two are of outstanding importance for the garden. One is *Scabiosa caucasica*, a
hardy herbaceous perennial, and the other is *S. atropurpurea*, a
plant invariably grown as an annual.

S. caucasica carries its large flat blue, mauve or white flowers
on stiff 2 to 3-foot stems and it blooms continuously from July
to October. It is not a plant that ever makes a great show at one
time, but it is excellent for cutting. It likes fairly well-drained,
but not dry, soils and open, sunny positions. It resents autumn
disturbance and should always be planted in spring and it can be
increased by careful division at that season.

S. atropurpurea is very different in appearance as the flowers
are bee-hive shaped and the colour range is much more varied,

from white and palest pink or mauve to an almost black purple. Seed can be sown in March in a frame or greenhouse, the seedlings being pricked out and hardened off for planting out in late May, or alternatively seed can be sown outdoors in April directly where the plants are to flower. This scabious grows about 3 feet high and should be spaced a foot apart.

SCHIZANTHUS *(Butterfly Flower)*

Among the most graceful of half-hardy annuals, the garden hybrids of *Schizanthus hybridus grandiflorus* have attractively marked flowers in shades of pink, mauve, purple, carmine, crimson and white with deeper markings of the ground colour or of yellow or bronze.

Best grown in the warm greenhouse, seed sown in John Innes compost in March or April in a temperature of 55° to 60° will produce plants to flower in August and September while seed sown in late August or early September will provide flowers in April or May. Seedlings should be potted on regularly until they reach 7, 8 or 9–inch pots in which they will flower. Growing tips should be pinched out when the plants are three or four inches high. Do not repot between November and February inclusive. Careful staking will be required, and cool, airy conditions are needed after germination. Water fairly freely in spring and summer, sparingly in autumn and winter.

SCILLA *(Bluebell, Squill)*

The common bluebell, *Scilla nonscripta*, needs no introduction, but it has a number of useful relatives that are not so well known. The one that most closely resembles it is the Spanish bluebell, *Scilla hispanica (campanulata)*. This is a more robust plant with broader leaves and taller, stiffer flower spikes. In addition to the blue form there are good pink and white varieties. It thrives under exactly the same conditions as our native bluebell and is a useful bulb to naturalize beneath shrubs.

Then there is the Siberian squill, *Scilla sibirica*, a much smaller plant with dainty spikes of bright blue flowers on 3 to 4–inch stems in March and April. It is a good bulb for the rock garden or for the front of the border and it likes sunny places.

By comparison *S. peruviana*, with its very broad spike of purple or white flowers, is a rather clumsy plant. It looks a little like a very squat and ungainly hyacinth.

All these scillas should be planted in autumn, 2 to 3 inches deep with the exception of the bluebell which can be as much as 6 inches deep. They can be increased by division of the bulb clusters.

SEDUM *(Stonecrop)*

The stonecrops are a large family of succulent plants most of which are hardy. They are useful for the rock garden and for walls and nearly all of them like warm sunny places. They vary a great deal in character from the completely prostrate *Sedum lydium* with tiny bronzy leaves to the 2–foot high *S. maximum*

Scabiosa
Columbaria

Schizanthus
pinnatus

Scilla
peruviana

Scilla
sibirica

111

*Sedum
sempervivoides*

*Sedum
acre*

*Sempervivum
arachnoideum*

*Sempervivum
soboliferum*

with quite large beetroot coloured leaves.

Two of the most popular stonecrops are *S. spathulifolium atropurpureum*, a prostrate spreading plant with thick, spoon-shaped leaves, plum-red in colour, and *S. spectabile* an 18-inch tall plant with large, flattish heads of pink flowers in early autumn. At that season it is one of the best plants for the front of the border.

There are a great many more kinds, mostly prostrate or low-growing plants which spread rapidly. All can be grown with the greatest of ease in almost any soil and open place. There is even one, *S. pulchellum*, with rosy-purple flowers, that likes rather moist soils and partially shaded positions. All can be increased by division in spring or autumn with the exception of *S. caeruleum* which is an annual and *S. pilosum* which is biennial. Both these must be renewed every year from seed.

SEMPERVIVUM (Houseleek)

The common houseleek, *Sempervivum tectorum*, got its name because of its ability to grow on the roofs of buildings with no more soil than might have been caught in the angle between one tile and another. In this respect it is a very typical member of its family for most of the sempervivums are happiest when spreading their stiff rosettes of leaves over the surface of a rock or the face of a wall. They all love, sun, warmth and good drainage and they can survive with a minimum of soil. They are grown primarily for their leaves which vary from the small, reddish, cobweb-covered rosettes of *Sempervivum arachnoideum* to the magnificent 8-inch bronze and red rosettes of *S. Boutignyanum*. Some, such as *S. calcareum* and *S. Greenii*, have grey-green leaves tipped with red and some, such as *S. tectorum* itself, are green throughout. All produce in summer, very stiff and solid flower spikes like little lighthouses, each bearing a cluster of starry pink or reddish flowers. They are curious rather than beautiful. All are hardy and perennial and all can be increased by division at almost any time of the year.

SENECIO (Groundsel, Cineraria)

The common groundsel is one of the most troublesome of garden weeds but it has some distinguished relatives that are first-rate garden or greenhouse plants. Probably the most popular of these is the plant that every gardener knows as cineraria but which the botanist calls *Senecio cruentus* (see Cineraria).

A very different plant is *Senecio laxifolius*. This is a hardy shrub 3 to 4 feet high with rounded grey leaves and masses of yellow daisy flowers in July. It likes warm, sunny places and fairly well-drained soils and is easily raised from cuttings of firm young shoots in July or August.

Yet another useful senecio is the dusty miller, *S. Cineraria*, a half-hardy, grey-leaved plant often used for summer bedding. It grows about 2 feet high and makes an admirable foil for the scarlet flowers of pelargoniums. It can be raised from cuttings of firm growth in spring or late summer.

SHORTIA

These are very beautiful, low growing perennials for the woodland or shady places in the rock garden. The two kinds usually seen are *Shortia galacifolia* and *S. uniflora*. Both are very similar, only a few inches high, and making wide clumps of shining green leaves from which appear in spring, fragile, bell shaped, pale pink flowers. They need cool leafy or peaty soil which is open enough to be well drained in winter and yet spongy enough to hold plenty of moisture in summer. They can be increased by careful division in spring. Also included in this family now as *S. soldanelloides* is the plant most gardeners know as *Schizocodon soldanelloides*. It needs similar treatment and has clusters of pale pink, fringed flowers in spring.

SIDALCEA

From the garden standpoint the most important sidalceas are the numerous varieties of *Sidalcea malvaeflora*, a hardy herbaceous perennial which carries slender spikes of pink flowers in summer. They are at their best in August. The varieties differ in height, varying from about 2 to 5 feet, and in colour from palest pink to near crimson. All are excellent border plants easily grown in any ordinary soil and reasonably open situation. They can be increased by division in spring or autumn.

SILENE *(Catchfly)*

There are both annual and perennial catchflies, the former usually being represented in British gardens by *Silene pendula*, a fragile plant with clusters of pale pink flowers in summer. It is a very easily grown plant, being quite hardy and not in the least fussy about soil. Sow it in March or April where it is to flower and thin the seedlings to a few inches apart.

The two most popular perennial kinds are *S. Schafta*, which makes a loose, tumbling mass of rather weedy growth which disappears in late summer beneath a cloud of rose-pink flowers, and *S. alpestris* which makes much neater tussocks of shining green leaves on which stand the small white flowers on slender 6–inch stems in June and July. *S. acaulis* is even closer and more compact in habit and has stemless, pink flowers, but is shy about producing them. These are all plants for sunny places in the rock garden or dry wall and all can be increased by division in spring.

SISYRINCHIUM *(Blue-eyed Grass)*

The common name, blue-eyed grass, really only applies to two sisyrinchiums, *S. Bermudiana* and *S. angustifolium* (*anceps*) and is very appropriate to them as both make grass-like leaves from which small violet-blue flowers appear intermittently all the summer. They are not plants to make a fuss about but are useful for their foliage and long-flowering season. As they are no more than 1 foot in height, they are most suitable for the rock garden or the extreme front of the border.

H

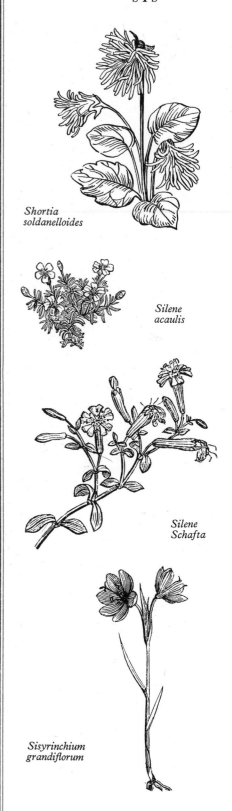

Shortia soldanelloides

Silene acaulis

Silene Schafta

Sisyrinchium grandiflorum

*Skimmia
japonica*

*Solanum
jasminoides*

*Solanum
macranthum*

*Solidago
Virgaurea*

Very different is *S. grandiflorum*, a beautiful but extremely fragile plant with rush-like leaves and nodding, silken-textured flowers, the colour of amethysts. There is also a white variety. This is a plant for a specially selected and sheltered place in the rock garden with well-drained soil and perhaps a pane of glass in April to protect its flowers from rain. Alternatively it can be grown in pots or pans in the alpine house.

All these sisyrinchiums can be increased by division in the spring.

SKIMMIA

The skimmias are compact evergreen shrubs which have the triple merits of good foliage, abundant white flowers and fine red berries. Moreover they are very easily grown in practically any soil and situation and they will even flower and berry quite well in shady places. The kind commonly grown, *Skimmia japonica*, suffers from the slight drawback that it has male and female flowers on separate plants and only the females will produce berries and then only if there is a male nearby to fertilize them. But there are other kinds which produce both sexes on the same bush, notably *S. Fortunei*, which is lower growing than *S. japonica*, usually not exceeding 2 feet, and *S. Foremanii* which reaches 3 to 5 feet as does *S. japonica*. All can be increased by layering in spring.

SOLANUM

The potato is a solanum but there are other species of the same genus which are grown solely for ornament. One of the best known of these is a greenhouse pot plant grown for its scarlet, cherry-like fruits at Christmas time. Its name is *Solanum Capsicastrum* and it is generally grown from seed sown in February or early March in a temperature of about 65°. The seedlings are potted singly, and repotted as necessary in John Innes compost. Pots 5 to 6 inches in diameter are usually large enough for the final potting in late May or early June. From June to September they are best plunged outdoors in a sunny sheltered place where they should be well watered, but by October they must be back in a greenhouse with an average temperature of 50°.

Another and very different kind is *S. crispum*, a vigorous climber for a sunny sheltered place. It will reach a height of 15 to 20 feet and it produces in summer, loose clusters of pale bluish-purple flowers not unlike those of the potato. Even more beautiful but a little more tender is *S. jasminoides* with similar habit and white flowers. These climbing solanums need no regular pruning and are increased by cuttings of young growth in spring in a propagating box with bottom heat.

SOLIDAGO *(Golden Rod)*

These are very easily grown hardy herbaceous perennials mostly flowering in late summer or early autumn and with fine sprays of small yellow daisy flowers. The commonest kind which is to be seen in almost every garden, is *Solidago canadensis*, which has

114

a great many garden varieties and hybrids with names such as Golden Wings, Golden Mosa and Leraft. These vary in height from 2 to 6 feet and in colour from pale to deep yellow. There is also a fine hybrid known as *S. missouriensis* (correctly *Solidaster luteus*) which is more rounded in habit, 2 to 3 feet high and lemon yellow in colour. All these golden rods will grow in almost any soil but prefer a sunny position. They can be increased very readily by division.

SPARTIUM *(Spanish Broom)*

Only one kind of Spanish broom is grown in gardens, *Spartium junceum*, a shrub with green, almost leafless stems, and slender spikes of bright yellow, sweetly scented pea-flowers from June to August. It likes sun and good drainage and does not seem to mind how poor the soil is, for which reasons it is often seen at its best near the sea. It will grow 8 or 10 feet high but can be kept a good deal shorter if it is pruned moderately each spring. The simplest method of increasing it is by seed sown in a frame in spring. This is in every way an outstanding member of the broom family for it is showy, easily grown and long flowering.

SPIRAEA

Most of the herbaceous plants that are familiarly known to gardeners as spiraea are, in fact, astilbes, and the true spiraeas are nearly all shrubs. There are some excellent kinds among them and they vary quite a lot in style. Two of the earliest and most popular are *Spiraea arguta* and *S. Thunbergii*, both making very twiggy bushes 4 to 6 feet high, smothered in April with tiny white flowers. A little later, in May, comes *S. Vanhouttei* which is a little stiffer but still very graceful in habit and carries its clusters of white flowers along the arching branches. One of the most useful kinds is *S. japonica*, especially in its variety Anthony Waterer. This makes a dense shrub with erect 4 to 5-foot stems terminated in July and August by flattish heads of pink flowers. These are carmine in Anthony Waterer and the leaves are usually flecked with cream. It is an ideal shrub for small gardens as it can be limited in size by a little careful cutting back each spring.

At the other extreme of size are *S. arborea* and the very similar *S. Lindleyana*. Both will grow 12 to 15 feet in height and produce great plumes of creamy white flowers in July and August. They are extremely handsome shrubs.

Another distinct group is represented by *S. Douglasii*, *S. Menziesii* and *S. salicifolia*, all of which have short bottle-brush-like spikes of fluffy pink flowers in late summer. They spread rather rapidly by suckers, which can be a nuisance, but they are fine, trouble-free shrubs for rough places.

Spiraea Aruncus, often known as goat's beard, is a very vigorous herbaceous plant which will grow 5 or 6 feet high and produce very fine plumes of creamy white flowers in June and July. Botanists no longer call it a spiraea but have named it *Aruncus sylvester*.

Spartium junceum

Spiraea japonica

Spiraea Douglasii

Spiraea Lindleyana

115

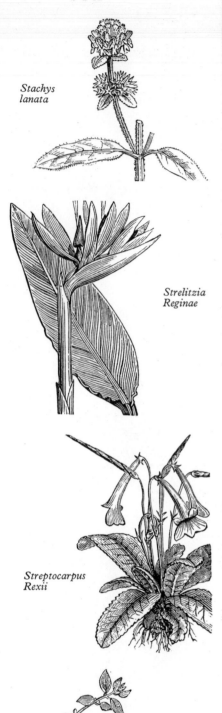

Stachys
lanata

Strelitzia
Reginae

Streptocarpus
Rexii

Symphoricarpos
albus

All shrubby spiraeas can be increased by cuttings of firm young stems in a frame in July or August and quite a number can also be increased by detaching suckers or offsets in autumn.

STACHYS *(Betony, Woundwort, Lamb's Ears)*

In general the betonys are not very choice garden plants but *Stachys lanata* has long been popular because of its extraordinarily soft and silky grey leaves. The spikes of reddish-purple flowers are also enveloped in grey down and it is this densely hairy nature that has earned it the popular name, lamb's ears. It is an indestructible hardy perennial which keeps close to the ground except when it throws up its 18–inch flower stems in summer. It will grow in any soil and reasonably open place and can be increased by division at practically any time of the year.

STRELITZIA *(Bird of Paradise Flower)*

The only species grown in gardens, *Strelitzia Reginae*, is one of the most extraordinary of all flowers. The flowers are shaped rather like the head of a bird with long purplish beak and a crest of orange and blue. These very handsome blooms are carried in May and June on long, stiff stems above leaves like those of a banana or very large canna. As might be expected this is a semi-tropical plant requiring warm greenhouse treatment in this country. It should be grown in large pots in John Innes compost and should be given a temperature of around 55° in winter rising to at least 65° from April onwards. It should be watered very freely from April to September and kept in a moist atmosphere but may be relatively dry in winter. Propagation is usually by division in spring.

STREPTOCARPUS *(Cape Primrose)*

The popular name of the streptocarpus is rather misleading for anything less like a primrose than this predominantly blue, trumpet-shaped flower it would be difficult to imagine. There are also pink and white varieties but yellow is conspicuous by its absence. Most of those grown in gardens are hybrids and all are greenhouse plants though they do not require high temperatures. They are usually raised from seed sown in a temperature of 65°, in January or February if the plants are to flower in early autumn, or in July if they are wanted in the summer. The seedlings are grown on in John Innes compost and are gradually worked on into 4 or 5–inch pots in which they will flower. They require a good deal of water while they are making rapid growth in spring and summer and at this period the atmosphere should also be kept as moist as possible, but in winter they need to be kept rather dry. An alternative method of propagation is by mature leaves pegged to a bed of sandy peat in a close frame with bottom heat. This can be done at almost any time in spring or summer.

SYMPHORICARPOS *(Snowberry)*

The common snowberry of British hedgerows is *Symphoricarpos albus (racemosus)*. It makes a dense bush of rather thin, twiggy growth and is notable for its globular white berries in autumn. At that season it is very decorative and though not, perhaps, a shrub for the more select parts of the garden it is well worth a place on the outskirts. It will thrive anywhere, even in competition with trees, and is a good cover shrub. There are other kinds less frequently seen, one of the best of which is *S. orbiculatus* often known as the coral berry on account of its rose-purple berries. Unfortunately it does not usually fruit sufficiently freely in this country to be effective. It should be given a warm and sunny situation. These shrubs can be increased by detaching offsets or suckers in autumn.

SYRINGA (Lilac)

The common lilacs are all derived from *Syringa vulgaris*, a tall shrub or small tree with pale purple flowers. The garden varieties have, in general, larger individual flowers and finer clusters, and they have a colour range from white and palest lavender to a deep reddish purple. There are single and double-flowered forms. In addition to these numerous varieties of common lilac, there are also several other species well worth growing, as well as hybrids between some of these species. There is, for example, the Hungarian lilac, *S. Josikae*, with elegantly formed clusters of lilac flowers. *S. reflexa* is a Chinese lilac which has small pink flowers in drooping clusters and *S. villosa*, which also comes from China, has very long flower clusters. A series of hybrids has been made between *S. reflexa* and *S. villosa* and these are often known as the Preston lilacs. They contain some very elegant and attractive shrubs with smaller flowers than those of the common lilac but more gracefully formed. *S. emodii* is very like *S. villosa*.

All these lilacs like fairly rich soils and open, sunny positions. They are quite hardy and easy to grow and they require no regular pruning. The species are easily raised from seed sown in spring in a frame, but the garden varieties do not come true to colour and form from seed and so are increased by grafting on to seedlings of the common lilac, by layering in spring or early summer, or by detaching suckers in autumn, if the plants are on their own roots and have not been grafted.

TAGETES (Marigold)

Not all the plants commonly called marigold belong to the tagetes family for the common pot marigold is a calendula, but the African marigold is *Tagetes erecta* and the French marigold is *T. patula*. There is also a very pretty little dwarf marigold with small single orange flowers which is named *T. signata pumila*. All these are annuals readily raised from seed sown in a greenhouse or frame in March. The seedlings should be pricked out as soon as possible into boxes of good soil, and should then be hardened off for planting outdoors in late May. All these marigolds like a sunny place. Though they will grow in almost any soil, for really good results the French and African varieties should have a rather rich soil—certainly a good deal richer than would be advisable for most annuals.

117

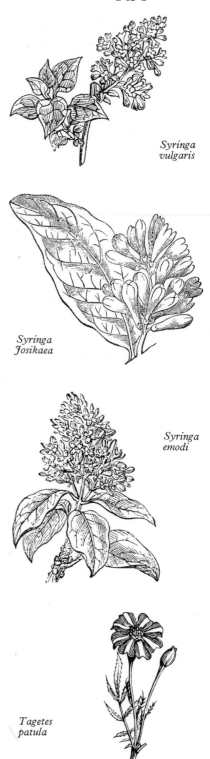

Syringa vulgaris

Syringa Josikaea

Syringa emodi

Tagetes patula

*Tamarix
gallica*

*Thalictrum
aquilegifolium*

*Thalictrum
minus*

*Thymus
Serpyllum*

The African marigolds are mostly between 2 and 3 feet tall and have very big, almost globular flowers in shades of yellow and orange. The French marigolds are shorter, usually about 18 inches, and they have rather smaller but more perfectly formed double flowers usually yellow with crimson or chestnut red markings.

TAMARIX *(Tamarisk)*

These very graceful shrubs thrive especially well near the seaside and are happiest in light, well-drained soils. All have very slender branches set with tiny green leaves not unlike those of heathers and their small flowers are produced in fine feathery plumes which are most graceful. One of the best is *Tamarix pentandra* which has pink flowers in August. There is also a variety of this named *rubra* in which the flowers are almost red. To extend the season there is *T. tetrandra* which bears its pink flowers in May. For finest results *T. pentandra* should be cut back hard each spring and *T. tetrandra* should be similarly pruned as soon as it has finished flowering. All species of tamarisk can be increased by cuttings of well ripened growth in autumn. *T. anglica* and *T. gallica* are frequently used for hedging in exposed sea side places.

THALICTRUM *(Meadow Rue)*

The loveliest of all the meadow rues is *Thalictrum dipterocarpum*, but it is not one of the easiest to grow. A rather tall herbaceous plant very sparsely branched and open in habit, it has small, round leaves and produces, in July and August, loose sprays of nodding lilac and yellow flowers. The effect of a well grown plant 5 or 6 feet high is very beautiful. There is also a double flowered form named Hewitt's Double. Both these plants need good but well-drained soils and rather warm positions. They are apt to be killed in winter on cold, wet soils.

Far easier to grow but not so graceful is *T. aquilegifolium* which has leaves very like those of a columbine (aquilegia) and clusters of small purplish flowers on 3-foot stems, in early summer. *T. glaucum* is rather taller and has pale yellow flowers and attractive grey foliage. *T. minus* (*adiantifolium*) is not above 18 inches high, has leaves like those of maidenhair fern and greenish yellow flowers in summer. All can be increased by careful division in spring.

THYMUS *(Thyme)*

The thymes are useful plants for the rock garden and also for the crevices between paving slabs. Several of them are quite prostrate in habit and of these one of the finest is *T. Serpyllum* and its numerous varieties. This makes a carpet of rooting stems set with tiny leaves and smothered in June and July by the heather-pink, carmine or white flowers. There is an attractive variety named *lanuginosus*, the leaves of which are clothed with whitish down. The lemon-scented thyme, usually sold as *T. citriodorus*, is in fact a variety of *T. Serpyllum*. It has an attractive golden leaved form. *T. nitidus* is one of the best of the erect, shrubby kinds, a neat, 18-inch high bush with grey-green, fragrant leaves and masses of soft pink flowers in May.

All thymes like well-drained soils and open sunny positions. The creeping kinds can be easily increased by division in spring but the shrubby kinds must be increased by cuttings of firm young shoots in July or August in a frame.

TIGRIDIA *(Tiger Flower)*

The tigridias are bulbous-rooted plants which are not quite hardy enough to be reliable outdoors except in the south and west. They like warm, sunny places and light, well-drained soils and are excellent plants for a sheltered border at the foot of a south wall. They are well worth a little trouble as they are extremely unusual and beautiful in flower. The species usually grown is *Tigridia Pavonia* which grows 2 to 2½ feet high and has widely opened flowers that look a little like three petalled tulips (there are actually six petals but three are very small). The colours are bright yellow, rose, red etc., usually spotted with a deeper colour. Though each flower only lasts a day, a succession of blooms is produced for several weeks in August. The corms should be planted in April and lifted in October and stored like those of gladioli.

TRADESCANTIA *(Spiderwort)*

Several of the tradescantias are greenhouse plants, one *Tradescantia fluminensis*, being a popular trailing plant for the edges of greenhouse stages or even for growing beneath the staging. It has several useful variegated varieties.

There is also one kind, *T. virginiana*, which is a perfectly hardy herbaceous perennial valuable for its long-flowering season and ability to thrive almost anywhere, in good soil or poor, sun or shade. It grows about 2 feet high, has broadly grass-like leaves and clusters of three-petalled flowers which open in succession from June to September. The wild species is purple-flowered but there are many garden varieties some of which are a clear lavender-blue or violet and some rose. All can be increased by division in spring or autumn.

TRILLIUM *(Wood Lily)*

These are very beautiful plants for shady places and cool leafy, or peaty soils. They grow 12 to 18 inches tall and carry their broad green leaves in threes. The flowers are also three-petalled (or appear so). One of the best is *Trillium grandiflorum* with white to rose flowers. *T. erectum* is rather a dull purple and perhaps more interesting than beautiful and another with purple or green flowers is *T. sessile*. All can be increased by careful division in March. They flower in April or May.

TROLLIUS *(Globe Flower)*

The globe flowers resemble very large, almost globular buttercups and all flower in spring or early summer, though they often

119

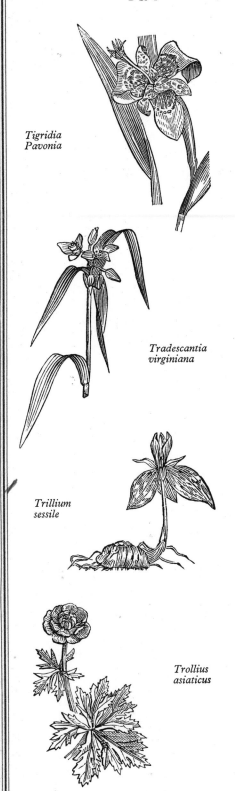

Tigridia Pavonia

Tradescantia virginiana

Trillium sessile

Trollius asiaticus

*Tropaeolum
speciosum*

*Tropaeolum
polyphyllum*

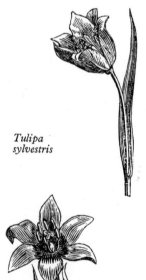

*Tulipa
sylvestris*

*Tulipa
Clusiana*

give a second flush of bloom in August. They like cool places and rather moist soils and though they can be grown in the herbaceous border they are really happier at the side of a stream or in damp soil near the edge of a bog garden. *Trollius europaeus* is the kind most commonly grown and this has numerous varieties or hybrids differing mainly in the precise shade of their flowers which may be anything from pale yellow to orange. All are about 2 feet high. *T. Ledebourii* is rather taller and flowers later, a further difference being that its orange flowers are more widely opened and less ball shaped. *T. asiaticus* is very much like *T. europaeus* and has colour forms varying from light to deep yellow. All can be increased by careful division in spring.

TROPAEOLUM *(Nasturtium)*

The popular annual which everyone knows as nasturtium is, in fact, *Tropaeolum majus*. This is a climbing plant in its natural form but it has a great many varieties some of which, like the Tom Thumb nasturtiums, are compact and bushy. All are plants of the easiest culture, growing in any soil however poor, and even tolerating shade, though they flower most freely in sunny places. The flowers are either yellow or some shade of red or crimson and are produced throughout the season. Though really quite tender *T. majus* grows so rapidly that it can be treated as a hardy annual by sowing the seed outdoors in April where it is to flower.

There are also fine perennial kinds of tropaeolum of which two of the best are *T. speciosum* (the flame flower) and *T. polyphyllum*. The first is a slender climber with small scarlet flowers in summer. It is a plant that likes to scramble up through an evergreen shrub such as a holly or rhododendron, which it will then drape with its gracefully divided leaves and vivid flowers. Though not a very hardy plant it does not like dry heat and does best in the damper parts of the country, especially in some parts of Scotland. *T. polyphyllum*, by contrast, loves sun and warmth and is a good plant for a sunny bank. It has a tuberous root and trailing stems set with grey-green leaves and bearing bright yellow flowers. It must be increased by seed but *T. speciosum* can be propagated by division of its roots.

TULIPA *(Tulip)*

The tulip is a plant which has been highly developed in cultivation over a period of several centuries and it is, therefore, not surprising that to-day there are thousands of varieties grouped in a dozen or more main classes. These range from the quite dwarf and very early Duc van Thol tulips which are really only suitable for forcing in the greenhouse, to the tall and late-flowering Darwins which are such favourites for bedding displays in May. The early-flowering tulips bloom in April and are further subdivided into single and double-flowered varieties. A little later come the Mendel and Triumph tulips which occupy an intermediate position between early-flowering and Darwin groups. Then in May, in addition to the Darwins, there are the so-called cottage tulips and their offshoot, the lily-flowered race. Cutting across these various groups are the parrot tulips which may be early or late but all of which have curiously twisted or slashed petals and colours usually splashed with green and contrasting shades in a very distinctive manner. An entirely new race of rather dwarf early-flowering tulips has been produced from *Tulipa Kauffmanniana* and another new race of tall late-flowering tulips with notably brilliant colours is being raised by hybridizing *Tulipa Fosteriana* with other groups. The Rembrandt tulips are Darwins with broken colours, i.e. one colour splashed or streaked on a base of another colour. There are also double May-flowering tulips which have flowers not unlike those of peonies.

All these beautiful types, with the exception of the Duc van Thols, can be grown outdoors in any reasonably good and well-drained soil. Their bulbs should be planted 4 or 5 inches deep in October or November and are best lifted again in July when the foliage has died down. They should then be stored in a cool dry place until planting time. Propagation is by division of the bulb clusters when they are lifted.

VENIDIUM

The best known species is *Venidium fastuosum*, a rather coarse annual about 3 feet high and bearing, in summer, large and immensely showy daisy flowers which are orange with a central zone of black. There are other kinds, such as *V. calendulacea* which is shorter and less strikingly marked and there are also many hybrids in a wide range of colours. Seed of all may be sown in a greenhouse or frame in March, the seedlings being pricked out and hardened off for planting out in May. *V. calendulacea* may also be treated as a hardy annual, seed being sown outdoors in April where the plants are to flower.

VERBASCUM *(Mullein)*

The mulleins are mostly rather tall plants with long, tapering spikes of flowers which may be yellow or buff coloured or, in *Verbascum phoeniceum*, purple. Some are good perennials but many are biennials or usually behave as such and these must be renewed from seed every year. This can be sown outdoors in May in a sunny place and well-drained soil. Among the best of the perennial kinds are *V. Chaixii*, *V. thapsiforme* (*densiflorum*) and *V. nigrum*, all of which are yellow and about 5 feet high, and various hybrids such as Cotswold Queen, buff; Gainsborough, lemon yellow; and Pink Domino, mauve. The common mullein, *V. Thapsus*, covered with grey hair, grows to 7 feet tall, but a better plant, equally woolly but shorter, is *V. Brousa*. All perennial kinds can be increased by root cuttings in a frame in winter.

VERBENA *(Vervain)*

The best known verbenas are the half-hardy trailing kinds used for summer bedding. These all have brilliantly coloured flowers in shades of red, pink, purple and violet. They are fine carpeting

121

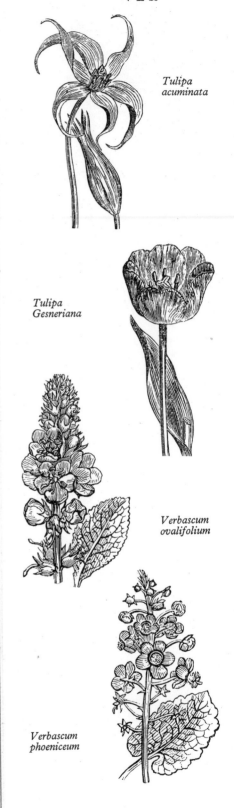

Tulipa acuminata

Tulipa Gesneriana

Verbascum ovalifolium

Verbascum phoeniceum

Verbena bonariensis

Verbena canadensis

Veronica spicata

Veronica speciosa

plants for sunny places and may also be grown on the top of terrace walls or in tubs, earthenware vases and hanging baskets. They are almost hardy and only require frame or cool greenhouse protection in winter. All can be readily raised from seed sown in a warm greenhouse in January or February, and selected forms can also be increased from cuttings taken in late summer and rooted in a frame.

In addition to these there are several hardy or near hardy kinds which may be grown in the herbaceous border or rock garden. *V. chamaedryfolia* has scarlet flowers, is a trailer and only thoroughly hardy in the milder parts of the country. *V. venosa* (*rigida*) is a good hardy perennial, a foot high, with close spikes of purple flowers from July to September, and *V. bonariensis* is a rather tall and sparse perennial with clusters of deep purplish blue flowers in August and September. All these can be increased by division in spring.

VERONICA *(Speedwell)*

There are both herbaceous and shrubby veronicas and botanists have separated most of the latter into a new genus under the name Hebe. However, as few gardeners have adopted this change, sensible though it seems, all the species are here treated as veronicas. All the shrubby kinds are evergreen and many of them are near the borderline of hardiness. Nevertheless there are such beautiful kinds among them that they are worth a little risk. *Veronica speciosa* is a late-flowering kind about 5 feet high which makes a shapely rounded bush and produces its short spikes of violet, purple, red or pink flowers from August to October. It does well by the seaside but is often severely damaged by frost inland. *V. salicifolia* has narrow leaves and slender, partially drooping spikes of white flowers from July to September. It is a very graceful evergreen but again is liable to be badly damaged by frost.

One of the hardiest is *V. Traversii*, a rounded, densely bushy shrub, 4 to 5 feet high with neat rounded leaves and short spikes of white flowers in July. Another very distinctive kind is *V. cupressoides*, a small shrub 18 to 24 inches high with such tiny leaves that it looks more like a conifer than a broad-leaved evergreen.

The herbaceous veronicas range from the completely prostrate, blue-flowered *V. rupestris*, an admirable carpeting plant for the rock garden, to the 6 foot tall, bluish-white *V. virginica*. *V. incana* has grey leaves and violet-blue flowers and is a good edging plant 9 to 12 inches high. *V. spicata* is taller, 1 to 2 feet, and it has slender spikes of blue, pink or white flowers. *V. longifolia subsessilis* is one of the best with fine spikes of blue-purple flowers in August and there are also several varieties of *V. latifolia*, 2 to 3 feet high, with narrow flower spikes which may be purple, pink or white.

All these herbaceous kinds are quite hardy and will grow in any ordinary soil and open position. They can be increased by division in spring or autumn. The shrubby kinds can be increased by cuttings of firm young growth in a frame at practically any time in summer or early autumn.

VIBURNUM *(Guelder Rose, Snowball Tree, Laurustinus)*

There are two viburnums that are called snowball trees because they have almost globular heads of white flowers. One of these is *Viburnum Opulus sterile*, a variety of the British guelder rose, and the other is *V. tomentosum plicatum*, often referred to as the Japanese snowball to distinguish it from the native kind. It has a very attractive habit, with horizontal branches, and the flower heads are not quite as large as those of *V. Opulus sterile*. There are also other varieties of *V. tomentosum* which have more or less flat heads of flowers borne all along the branches and these are quite as decorative as the globular headed varieties. All these flower in May and early June and are deciduous.

The popular laurustinus is *Viburnum Tinus* and is one of the best of evergreen winter flowering shrubs. It will grow 8 or 10 feet high and makes a very dense, rounded bush. The flower heads are pale pink in bud, white when open and they continue from January to April.

Another fine winter-flowering kind, this time deciduous, is *V. fragrans*, a rather stiffly branched shrub, 8 to 10 feet high which produces its small clusters of very fragrant white, pink-tinged flowers from November to February. It is perfectly hardy and even its flowers will survive a considerable amount of frost. In April and May comes *V. Carlesii*, another very fragrant shrub with clusters of white, pink-tinted flowers. It grows 5 or 6 feet high.

V. rhytidophyllum is an evergreen worth growing for its large, deep green leaves which have a remarkably wrinkled surface. It makes a big shrub, 10 or 12 feet high and carries large trusses of rather dull whitish flowers in June which are followed by red berries. There is an attractive variety in which the flower buds are pink.

All these viburnums will grow in any reasonable soil. They can be increased by cuttings of firm young shoots in July or August.

VINCA *(Periwinkle)*

The periwinkles are creeping evergreen shrubs which are useful for ground cover in shady places. They do well on banks or beneath trees that are not too closely planted, and they all flower in spring. The two principal kinds are *Vinca major* and *V. minor* but the latter is more useful as a garden plant as it has produced a number of varieties some with single and some with double flowers, a colour range from white and palest blue to purple and rose, and at least two forms with variegated leaves. All are of the easiest cultivation in almost any soil that does not dry out too much. They are naturally woodland or hedgerow plants and these are the conditions that suit them. They can be increased by division of the roots in autumn.

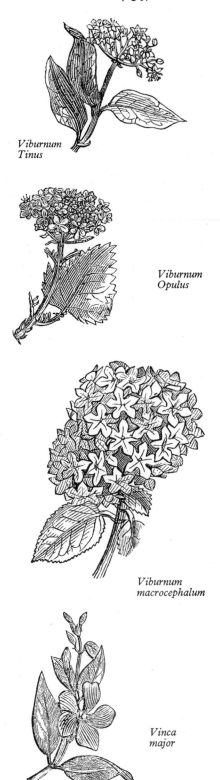

Viburnum
Tinus

Viburnum
Opulus

Viburnum
macrocephalum

Vinca
major

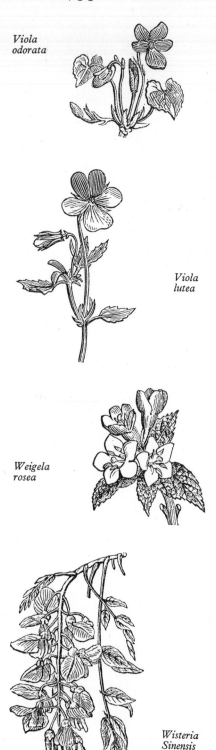

*Viola
odorata*

*Viola
lutea*

*Weigela
rosea*

*Wisteria
Sinensis*

VIOLA *(Pansy, Violet)*

The common bedding viola, the pansy and the violet are all members of the same genus, known to botanists as Viola. This can be a trifle muddling to the gardener until he gets used to it. The bedding viola is a good perennial which can be propagated either by careful division of the roots in spring or by cuttings of young shoots in early autumn. It will grow almost anywhere but likes best rather good, porous soils that contain enough humus to keep them cool and moist even in warm weather. It has tufted growth and is an ideal plant for edging or for making a carpet beneath taller plants. The flowering season is from May to September and the colour range includes almost everything except red.

Pansies differ from violas in being more straggly and less tufted in growth, in having flowers usually with strong markings, often black on yellow, purple, blue or bronze, and being less reliable perennials. They can be increased by cuttings as for violas but it is common practice to renew them annually from seed sown in a frame or greenhouse in February or March. The seedlings are pricked out and hardened off for planting out in good soil in May.

Violets are divided into single and double-flowered varieties, the latter being less vigorous and more difficult to grow. All thrive in fairly rich soils well supplied with moisture though not badly drained. They can be increased by careful division in spring but a better method is to make cuttings from the runners in early autumn and root them in a frame. They are planted out in good soil the following April and will make sturdy clumps for flowering the following winter.

WEIGELA

These very decorative deciduous shrubs are sometimes known in gardens by an alternative but discarded botanical name, Diervilla. All make rather large well-branched shrubs which tend to become arching in habit with age. The trumpet shaped flowers are borne in small clusters all along the stems and make a very fine display in late May and June. Often there is a second lot of flowers in late summer. Most of the varieties cultivated are hybrids. Among the best are Abel Carriere, pink, Eva Rathke and Newport Red, both deep carmine, and *styriaca*, rose. All will grow in practically any soil and situation but prefer one that is fairly sunny. They do not need regular pruning but flowering branches can be cut back when the flowers fade. All can be increased by cuttings of half-ripe shoots in a frame in July or by firmer cuttings outdoors in autumn.

WISTERIA

These are among the loveliest and most popular of hardy climbing plants. There are several kinds, all very vigorous and producing long, trailing spikes of soft lavender or mauve flowers in May and early June. The most popular is *Wisteria sinensis*, the Chinese wisteria, but *W. floribunda*, the Japanese wisteria, has

*Yucca
gloriosa*

*Yucca
filamentosa*

*Zinnia
tenuiflora*

*Zinnia
elegans*

longer flower trails, particularly in its variety *macrobotrys* in which they may be as much as 3 feet. There are several other varieties of this wisteria, one with pale pink flowers, and there are white flowered forms of both the Chinese and Japanese wisterias.

All like good soils and warm sunny places. They are happiest trained against a sunny wall but may also be grown over pergolas or can even be trained in the open to form standards or large bushes. Though regular pruning is not essential it is often convenient to shorten sidegrowths to four or five leaves each July. The best method of increase is by layering the long stems in early summer.

YUCCA *(Adam's Needle)*

The yuccas are all very exotic looking plants with stiff rosettes of long, sword-shaped leaves, sometimes carried almost on the ground, as in *Yucca filamentosa* or *Y. flaccida*, and sometimes carried on a short trunk as in *Y. gloriosa*. The flowers are creamy white and produced in July or August, in long erect spikes which have a very striking appearance. It is often stated that they take a great many years to flower but this is quite incorrect as plants that are growing well in a warm, sunny place and reasonably good but well-drained soil, usually flower quite regularly every year.

Most of the species are not too hardy and are most suitable for the mild southern and western counties or for seaside gardens, but *Y. filamentosa* and *Y. flaccida* usually succeed quite well in most parts of the country. In very cold places the leaves may be tied together in early winter to form a tent-like protection to the heart of the rosette. Yuccas are increased by seeds sown in a greenhouse in spring and also by rooted offsets detached in March.

ZINNIA *(Youth and Old Age)*

These very popular and brightly coloured, half-hardy annuals need to be sown a little later than most other plants of this class. Sow in a cool greenhouse in late March or an unheated frame in early April and grow straight on without either check or forcing. In too much heat the seedlings are apt to damp off. Zinnias like good soils and warm, sunny places. They grow about 3 feet high and should be spaced at least a foot, preferably 18 inches, apart. For late summer flowers it is wise to sow some seeds in early May directly in the open ground where they are to bloom and to thin the seedlings to the necessary distance.

There are several different types of zinnia. The best known is the large-flowered type with rather broad, flat petals, making an almost ball-like flower. A more recent development is the chrysanthemum-flowered type in which the petals are rolled and the bloom has a spiky appearance. There is also a race of pompon or miniature-flowered zinnias. All have the full zinnia range of colours including particularly strong reds and crimsons, fine yellows, pink and rose shades.

125

INDEX

to popular and catalogue names